Frederick Westlake

The Popular Hymn and Tune Book, for One, Two, Three and Four Voices

With accompaniment : containing a large variety of hymns and sacred songs for general use, and for every occasion throughout the yeara

Frederick Westlake

The Popular Hymn and Tune Book, for One, Two, Three and Four Voices
With accompaniment : containing a large variety of hymns and sacred songs for general use, and for every occasion throughout the yeara

ISBN/EAN: 9783337393847

Printed in Europe, USA, Canada, Australia, Japan

Cover: Foto ©Thomas Meinert / pixelio.de

More available books at **www.hansebooks.com**

The Popular Hymn and Tune Book,

FOR ONE, TWO, THREE, AND FOUR VOICES,

With Accompaniment;

CONTAINING

A LARGE VARIETY OF HYMNS AND SACRED SONGS FOR GENERAL USE,

AND FOR EVERY OCCASION THROUGHOUT THE YEAR;

IN WHICH ARE INCLUDED

A NUMBER OF EASY MELODIES

SUITED FOR SCHOOLS AND ELEMENTARY USE.

EDITED BY

FREDERICK WESTLAKE,

ASSOCIATE OF THE ROYAL ACADEMY OF MUSIC.

LONDON: BURNS AND OATES.
NEW YORK: CATHOLIC PUBLICATION SOCIETY CO.

ADVERTISEMENT.

As the present publication is intended to furnish a supply of Music for general use, it will be found to contain a variety of pieces fitted for schools and elementary purposes, as well as for the use of more advanced singers. With so wide a scope, it has of course been found necessary, in many cases, to set the same Hymns to Music of different styles, leaving the instructor or teacher to choose that which he finds most suited for his singers. By way of affording some guide, however, a Table has been given, at the end of the Index, of the Melodies most desirable to begin with, where Music of a very easy and popular character is required.

For more practised singers, a choice may be made from the many beautiful Hymns arranged by their Composers in Vocal Parts, which may be sung either with or without accompaniment. The verses may be sung in these two ways alternately; or again, the plan of singing one verse in unison with a large body of voices, and the alternate verse in harmony by a select number, may be adopted,—thus combining in an agreeable manner the two departments of Choir and Popular Singing. Where Hymns of this kind are used, as is often the case, for filling up intervals, such as before Sermons, Benediction, &c., this mode of performance would be found especially desirable.

It remains to be added, that a good deal of variety may be produced, as well as different tastes and purposes accommodated, by an interchange of Hymns and Tunes. For example, there are a great number of Melodies for such ordinary measures as "Jesus, the very thought of Thee;" "My God, how wonderful Thou art;" "Come, O Creator, Spirit blest;" "Look down, O Mother Mary;" "Hail, bright Star of Ocean;" "Jesus, gentlest Saviour;" &c. &c. These may be selected from at the option of the Choirmaster, who will also have no difficulty in finding appropriate Music for any words not included in this book.

INDEX.

N.B. A large proportion of the Music in this Volume is original, and composed expressly for the work.

A	No.
Adeste fideles	71, 234
Again the holy morn	128
Again the slowly circling year	94
Agony, The	87
All ye who seek a sure relief	80, 288
An exile for the faith	78
As fades the glowing orb of day	134, 275, 285
At last Thou art come, little Saviour	28
At the Cross her station keeping	158, 236, 281
Ave Verum	51

B	
Blest is the faith divine and strong	21
Blest Three in One	58

C	
Christian soul, dost thou desire	122
Christians, to the war	235
Christ the Lord is risen to-day	88, 88A, 189
Come, all ye faithful	71, 234, 273
Come, Holy Ghost, Creator, come	94, 97
Come, Holy Ghost, Thy grace inspire	98
Come, Holy Ghost, send down those beams	98
Come, Holy Spirit, from the height	65
Come, O Creator, Spirit blest	17, 96, 248, 273
Come, ye little children	43
Creator of the starry frame	67
Creator Spirit, by whose aid	66
Crown Him, the Virgin's Son	64

D	
Daily, daily sing to Mary	10, 31, 244
Daughter of God the Father	42
Dear Angel, ever at my side	223, 241, 6, 7
Dear little One, how sweet Thou art	6, 72
Dear Lord, who in Thy love so great	129
Dear husband of Mary	29

E	
Exult, all hearts, with gladness	63

F	
Faith of our fathers	33, 198
Fly hither from the storm	124
From circlets starred with many a gem	77
From pain to pain	230
From the highest heights of glory	202, 183
Full in the panting heart of Rome	40
Full of glory, full of wonders	59

G	No.
Glory be to Jesus	162, 8
God bless our Pope	40
God of mercy and compassion	83, 222
Green are the leaves	239
Great God, whatever through Thy Church	246

H	
Hail, bright Star of Ocean	168, 169, 250, 251
Hail, Cross most sweet and holy	160
Hail, Gabriel, hail	204
Hail, glorious St. Patrick	11, 15
Hail, holy Joseph, hail	14, 191, 220, 254, 283
Hail, Jesus, hail	20, 161
Hail, Ocean Star	216
Hail, Queen of Heaven	1, 173, 243
Hail, thou resplendent Star	177
Hail, true Body of the Saviour	51
Hail, wounds, which through eternal years	77
Happy we who, thus united	221, 244
Hark, an awful voice is sounding	68, 268
Hark, hark, my soul	22, 139
Have mercy on us, God most high	54, 55, 247
Have mercy on me	50
Hear Thy children, gentlest Jesus	179, 221
Hear thy children, gentlest Mother	179, 49
Heart of the Holy Child	44, 228
Heaven is the prize	149
Help, Lord, those souls which Thou hast made	227
Holy Ghost, come down upon Thy children	35
Holy Godhead, One in Three	60
Holy Mother, pierce me through	236
Holy Queen, we bend before thee	183, 253
Holy Spirit, Lord of light	65, 233
How gently flow the silent years	118

I	
I dwell a captive in this heart	147, 118
I'll never forsake thee	225
I love Thee, O Thou Lord most high	116
I met the Good Shepherd	9
Immaculate, immaculate	24
In Christ's dear name	113
In heaven 'tis given to rest thee	145
In this sweet Sacrament	211
It is my sweetest comfort	75
I was wandering and weary	27
I worship thee, sweet Will of God	23, 118

INDEX.

J

	No.
Jerusalem, thou city blest	101
Jesu, Creator of the world	69, 17, 18, 270
Jesu, my soul hath in Thy love	70
Jesus, all hail, who for my sin	81
Jesus, as though Thyself wert here	85
Jesus, ever-loving Saviour	47
Jesus, gentlest Saviour	8, 168, 270
Jesus is God	61
Jesus, let me call Thee Son	218
Jesus, Lord, be Thou my own	104, 122
Jesus, my Lord, my God, my all	206, 207
Jesus, my Lord, behold at length the time	25
Jesus, the very thought of Thee	2, 107, 141, 255, 106
Jesus, to Thee we look	78, 192
Joy, joy, the Mother comes	156, 191
Joys and glories of heaven	102

K

Kind Angel Guardian	16, 17, 18
Knowest thou, sweet Mary	162

L

Lead me to Thy peaceful manger	155
Let those who seek the world to please	13
Let those who will for other beauties pine	111
Light of the anxious heart	103
Light of the soul, O Saviour blest	108, 17, 18, 125, 265
Like the dawning of the morning	182, 163
Look down, O Mother Mary	177, 178, 279
Lord of eternal truth	58
Lovely flowers of martyrs	193
Loving Shepherd of the sheep	104

M

Majesty divine	59
Mary, thy heart for love	57
Michael, prince of highest heaven	205
Miserere	50
Mother Mary, at thine altar	215, 179, 221
Mother of mercy, day by day	172, 213, 252
Mother of our Lord and Saviour	193
My God, how wonderful Thou art	4, 52, 53, 151
My God, I love Thee	249, 53
My God, O Goodness Infinite	62A, 114
My Jesus, say what wretch has dared	159
My Lord, my God, what willest Thou	113
My Shepherd is the living God	115
My soul, what dost thou	209

N

None of all the noblest cities	74, 282
Now are the days of humblest prayer	231
Now at the Lamb's high royal feast	90
Now doth the fiery sun	263
Now doth the sun ascend the sky	127
Now let the earth with joy resound	277
Now with the fast-departing light	136, 250, 284

O

O balmy and bright	174
O blest Creator of the light	131, 261, 267, 287
O blessed Father, sent by God	199, 4, 5, 181
O Bread of Heaven	210
O Brightness of eternal light	129
O come and mourn with me awhile	157, 237
O come to the merciful Saviour	121
O Christ, Thy guilty people spare	203, 17, 18, 271
O'erwhelm'd in depths of woe	76, 240
O Father, Son, and Holy Ghost	150
O flower of grace, divinest flower	226
O flowers! O happy flowers	258
Oft, my soul, thyself remind	148
O God of orphans, hear our prayer	152, 152A
O God of loveliness	57
O Godhead hid, devoutly I adore Thee	238
O God, Thy power is wonderful	52A
O heavenly Jerusalem	100
O Jesus, God and man	256
O Jesus, Jesus, dearest Lord	7, 256
O Jesu, joy of loving hearts	105
O Jesu, King most wonderful	62
O Jesu, my beloved King	140
O Jesu, our Redemption	79
O Jesu, Saviour of the world	16, 17, 18, 269
O Jesu, Thou the beauty art	5, 70, 117
O King of heaven	23
O Lord of light	201
O Lord of perfect purity	125
O lovely voices of the sky	73, 214
O Maid conceived without a stain	214
O Mary, my Mother	38
O Mother blest	181
O Mother, I could weep for mirth	24
O Paradise, O Paradise	45, 46
O purest of creatures	15, 212
O Sion, open wide thy gates	75
O sing a joyous carol	12
O soul of Jesus, sick to death	87, 237
O Thou eternal King most high	92, 92A
O Thou in whom our love doth find	93, 129
O Thou, of all Thy warriors Lord	278
O Thou, the martyrs' glorious King	18, 194, 229, 242
O Thou, true life of all that live	262, 286
O turn to Jesus, Mother, turn	180, 85, 237
O vision bright, O land of light	39, 176
O what is this splendour	142, 15
O what is this enchanting calm	237
O why art thou sorrowful	120
O ye who seek the Lord	78

P

Pilgrims of the night	22, 139
Praise we our God with joy	56
Praise ye the Lord, on every height	109

R

Raise your voices, vales and mountains	184
Rise, glorious Victor, rise	91
Rosary: Joyful Mysteries	186, 187
,, Sorrowful	188, 104
,, Glorious	85, 130, 169

INDEX.

S

	No.
Saint of the Sacred Heart	195
See, amid the winter's snow	154, 144
Seek ye the grace of God	192
Sing, sing, ye angel bands	26, 166
Sleep, holy Babe	32, 153, 153A
Slumber, haste on dewy pinions	49
Snow and rain have vanished	41
Soon the fiery sun ascending	89
Soul of Jesus, make me holy	84
Spotless Anna, Judah's glory	171
Star of Jacob, ever beaming	170, 171, 183
Sweet Agnes, holy child	228
Sweet morn, thou parent of the sun	214
Sweet Saviour, bless us ere we go	132, 133, 175, 210, 266

T

	No.
That day of wrath, that dreadful day	85
The darkness fleets, and joyful day	129
The day, the happy day, is dawning	34
The glory of summer is faded and fled	224
The heathen monarch sits enthroned	197
The joyous birds are singing	190
The moon is in the heavens above	175, 243
The Mother sits, all-worshipful	164
There is one true and only God	245, 274, 4
The shadows of the evening hours	135, 110, 272
The snow lay on the ground	48
The star that heralds in the morn	126
The sun is sinking fast	138
The west'ring sun rolls down	137
They whom we loved on earth	119
Thou Crown of all the virgin choir	200, 17
Thou loving Maker of mankind	86, 237, 259
Thy home is with the humble, Lord	123
'Tis Thy good pleasure, not mine own	110
To Christ, the Prince of Peace	82, 192, 289
To Jesu's Heart, all burning	36, 37

U

	No.
Uplift the voice and sing	167

W

	No.
Wave the sweet censer, wave	91
We come to Thee, sweet Saviour	30
What light is streaming from the skies	19, 17, 264
When morning gilds the skies	276
When the loving Shepherd	208, 280
Who can paint that lovely city	102
Why is thy face so lit with smiles	3, 163

Y

	No.
Ye sons and daughters of the Lord	232

NOTE.

The following Melodies among others will be found suitable for elementary purposes:

1	15	49	130	177	248
2	16	67	141	186	250
4	17	72	149	214	251
7	33	90	168	241	252
8	36	94	171	242	257
10	47	122	172	243	263

Hymns and Sacred Songs.

Part I.

CONTAINING

EASY HYMNS, CHIEFLY FOR UNISON SINGING,

WITH ACCOMPANIMENT.

1. HAIL, QUEEN OF HEAVEN!

Words in "Hymns for the Year," No. 119.

2.

Words in "Hymns for the Year," No. 110.

4.

Words in "Hymns for the Year," No. 3.

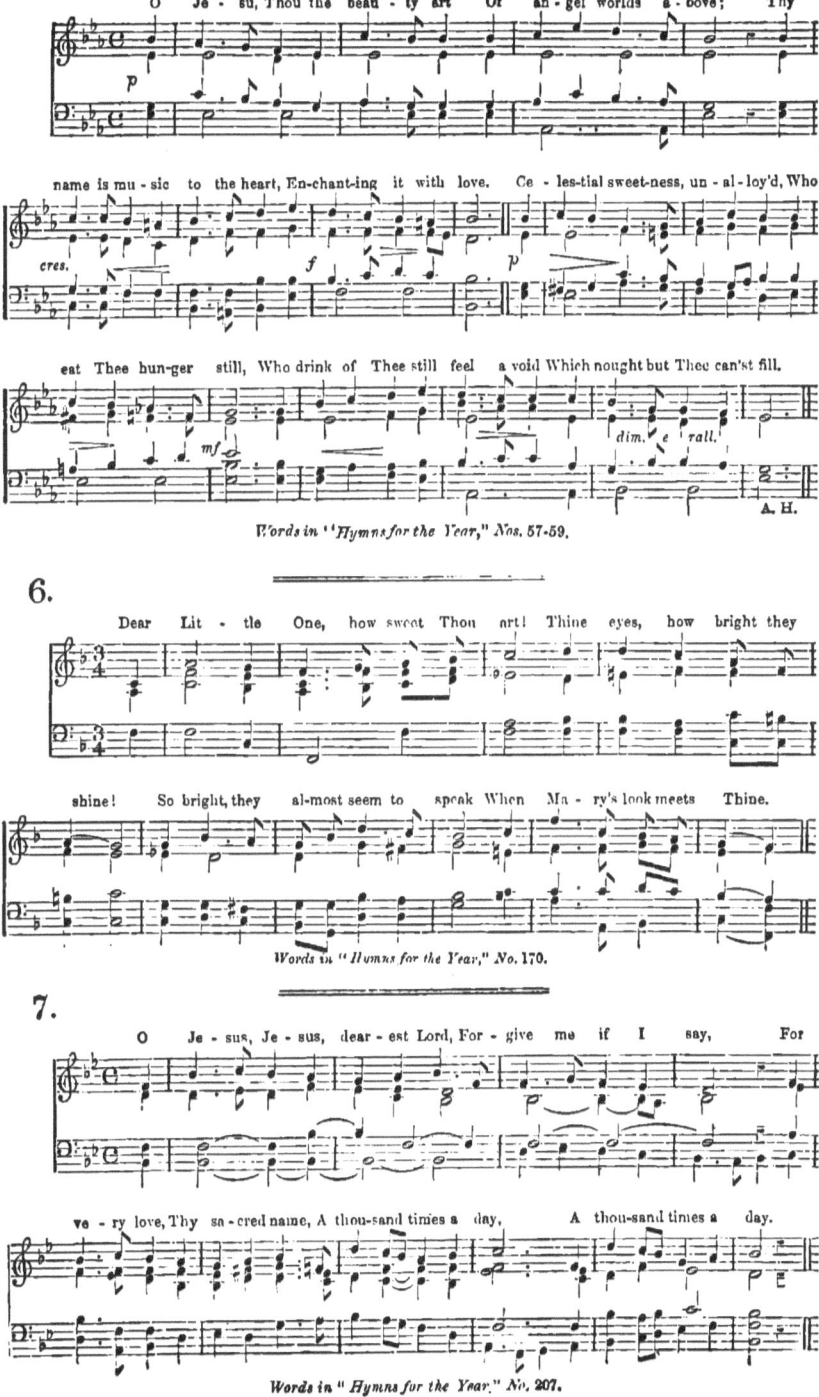

8. ## JESUS, GENTLEST SAVIOUR!
(Thanksgiving after Communion.)

Words in "Hymns for the Year," No. 166.

F. W.

9. ## THE GOOD SHEPHERD.

THE GOOD SHEPHERD—*(continued).*

sa-ving Thy sheep; Thy rai-ment all o-ver with crim-son is dyed, And what is this rent they have
fall-en on Thee? Oh, then, let me strive, for the love Thou hast borne, To give Thee no long-er oc-

made in Thy side?
ca-sion to mourn.

Words in "*Hymns for the Year,*" No. 99.

W. S.

10. DAILY, DAILY, SING TO MARY.

Dai-ly, dai-ly, sing to Ma-ry, Sing, my soul, her prai-ses due; All her feasts, her ac-tions, wor-ship, With the heart's de-vo-tion true. Lost in won-d'ring con-tem-pla-tion, Be her ma-jes-ty con-fest. Call her Mo-ther, call her Vir-gin, Hap-py Mo-ther, Vir-gin blest.

Words in "*Hymns for the Year,*" No. 132.

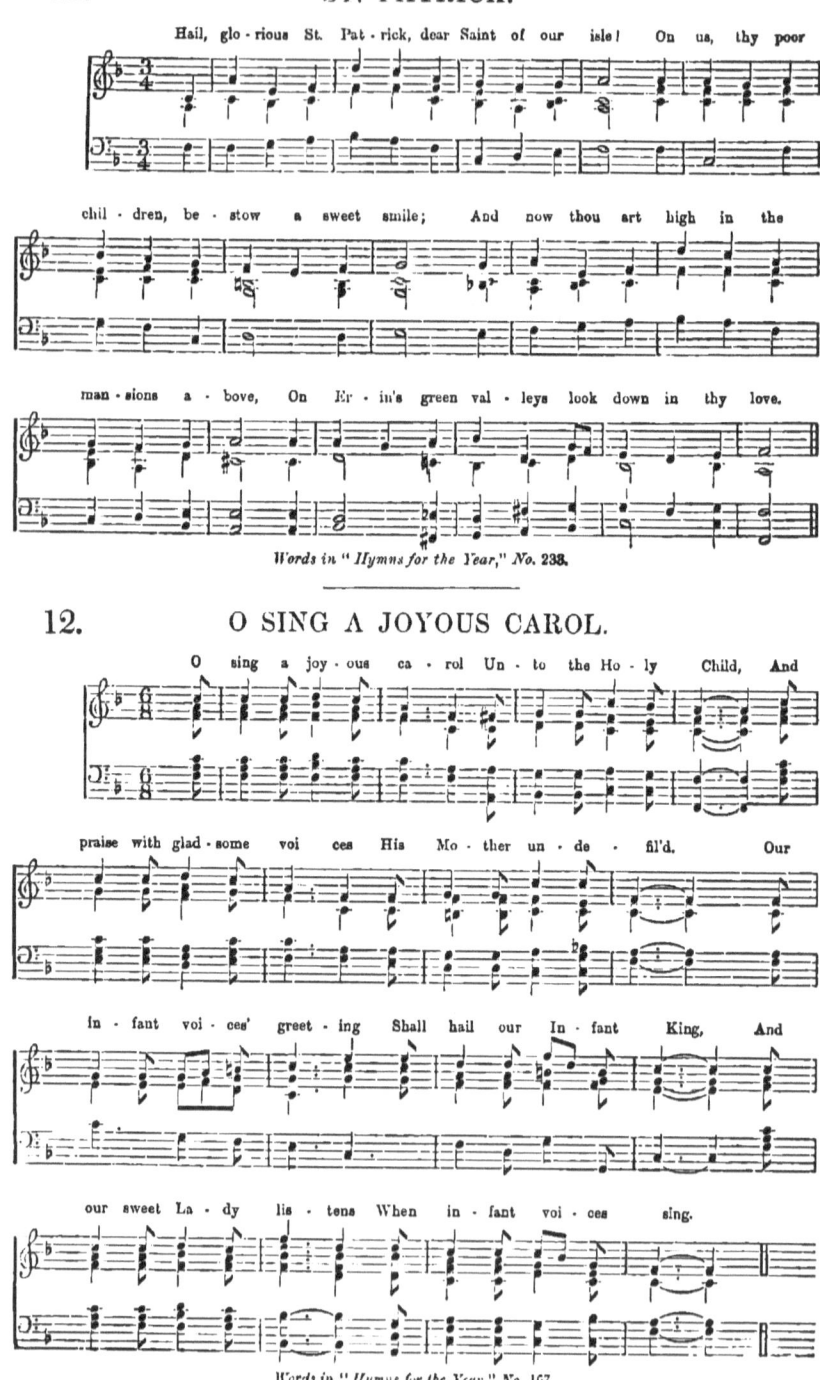

13. LET THOSE WHO SEEK THE WORLD TO PLEASE.

(Holy Family Hymn.)

Let those who seek the world to please, Do all for honour, wealth, and ease;
But in the Holy Family A nobler motive far have we:
CHORUS. Living, we will say, joyfully each day, "All for Jesus, Mary, Joseph;"
Dying, we will cry, till our latest sigh, "All for Jesus, Mary, Joseph!"

Words in "Hymns for the Year," No. 136.

14. HAIL, HOLY JOSEPH!

Hail, holy Joseph, hail! Chaste spouse of Mary, hail!
Pure as the lily flow'r In Eden's peaceful vale.

Words in "Hymns for the Year," No. 140.

Words in "Hymns for the Year," No. 127.

The four following Melodies are in the same measure, and may be used for any appropriate Hymns.

 16.

Words in "Hymns for the Year," No. 189.

20. THE PRECIOUS BLOOD.

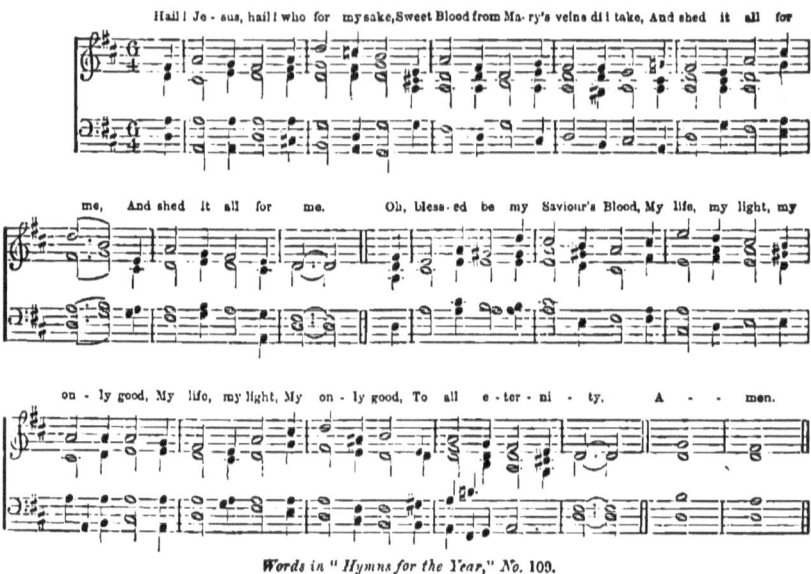

Words in "Hymns for the Year," No. 109.

21. BLEST IS THE FAITH.

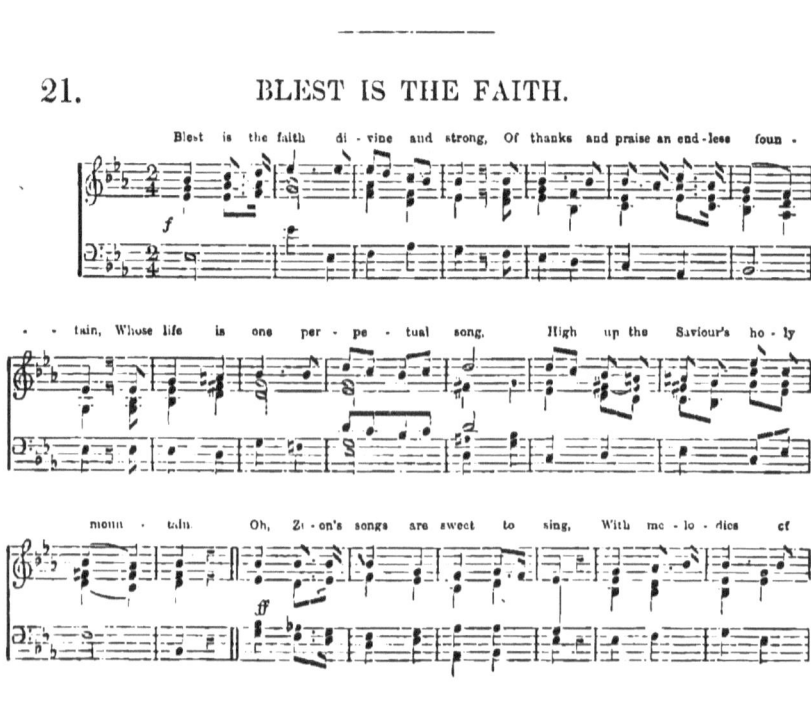

23. O KING OF HEAVEN!

(*Christmas Song.*)

Words in "*Hymns for the Year,*" No. 172.

24. IMMACULATE.

Words in "*Hymns for the Year,*" No. 192.

25. HYMN OF REPENTANCE.

Words in "Hymns for the Year," No. 185.

26. SING, SING, YE ANGEL-BANDS.

Words in "Hymns for the Year," No. 114.

Words in "Hymns for the Year," No. 182.

28. AT LAST THOU ART COME, LITTLE SAVIOUR.

(Christmas Hymn.)

AT LAST THOU ART COME, LITTLE SAVIOUR—(continued).

Words in "Hymns for the Year," No. 169.

29. THE PATRONAGE OF ST. JOSEPH.

Words in "Hymns for the Year," No. 174.

30. WE COME TO THEE, SWEET SAVIOUR.

We come to Thee, sweet Saviour, Just be-cause we need Thee so; None need Thee more than we do, None are half so vile or low. O beau-ti-ful sal-va-tion! O life e-ter-nal won! O plen-ti-ful re-demp-tion! O blood of Ma-ry's Son! O blood of Ma-ry's Son!

Words in "Hymns for the Year," No. 208.　　　　W. S.

31. DAILY, DAILY SING TO MARY.

Dai-ly, dai-ly sing to Ma-ry, Sing, my soul, her prai-ses due; All her feasts her ac-tions wor-ship, With the heart's de-vo-tion

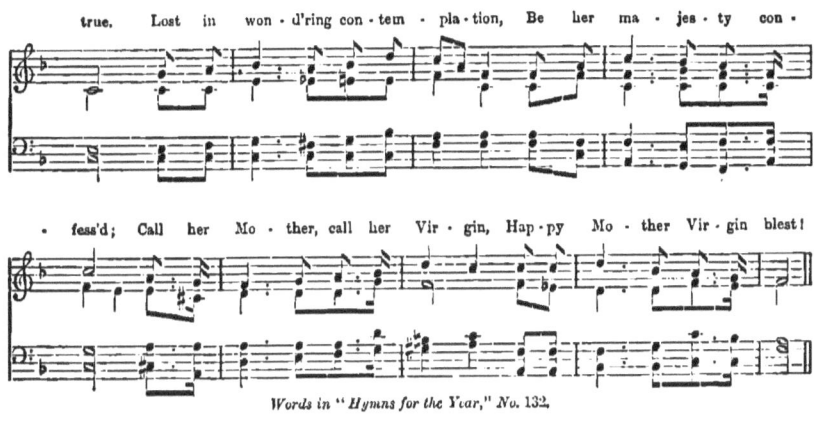

Words in "Hymns for the Year," No. 149.

34. THE DAY, THE HAPPY DAY, IS DAWNING.

(Feast of the Immaculate Conception.)

Words in "Hymns for the Year," No. 123.

35. HOLY GHOST, COME DOWN UPON THY CHILDREN.

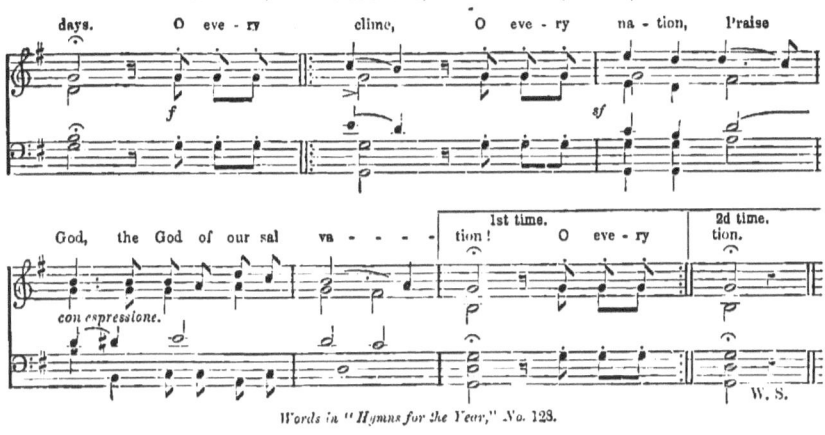

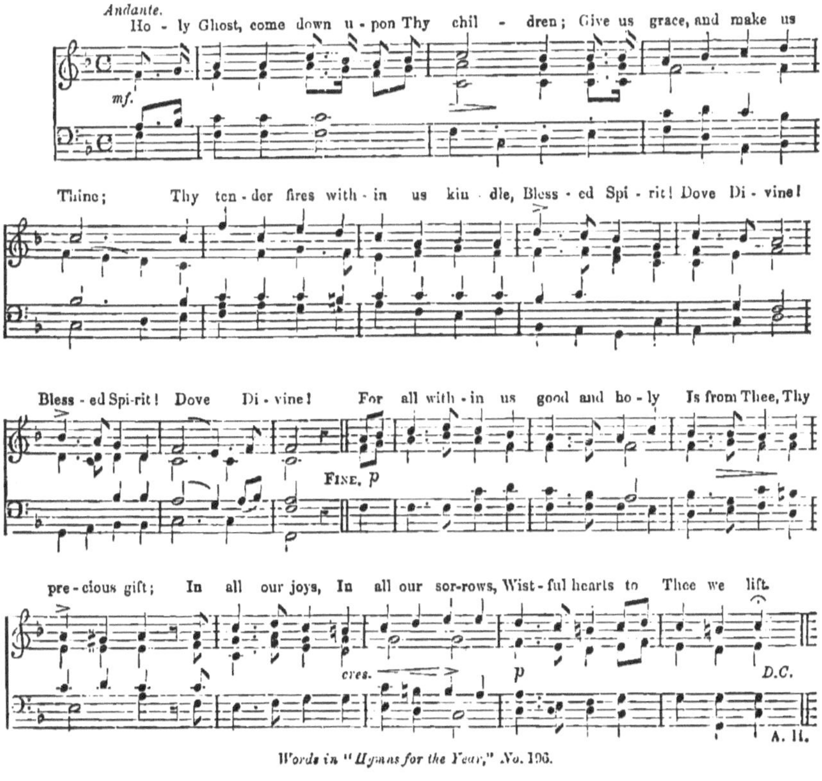

Words in "Hymns for the Year," No. 196.

36. TO JESUS' HEART ALL BURNING.

To Je-sus' Heart all burn-ing With fer-vent love for men, My heart with fond-est yearn-ing Shall raise its joy-ful strain. While a-ges course a-long, Blest be with loud-est song The sa-cred Heart of Je-sus By ev'-ry heart and tongue, Blest be the Heart of Je-sus By ev'-ry heart and tongue. A-men.

Words in "*Hymns for the Year,*" No. 206.

37. TO JESUS' HEART ALL BURNING.

To Je-sus' Heart all burn-ing, With fer-vent love for men, My heart with fond-est yearn-ing Shall raise its joy-ful strain. While

TO JESUS' HEART ALL BURNING.

Words in "*Hymns for the Year*," No. 206.

38. O MARY, MY MOTHER.

39. O VISION BRIGHT!

Words in "Hymns for the Year," No. 122.

40. GOD BLESS OUR POPE!

GOD BLESS OUR POPE!—(continued.)

Words in "Hymns for the Year," No. 239.

41 SNOW AND RAIN HAVE VANISH'D.

Words in "Hymns for the Year," No. 177.

42. SALUTATIONS TO MARY.

Daugh-ter of God the Fa-ther, O Vir-gin pure and mild, I ve-ne-rate and love thee, O take me for thy child! My soul and all its pow-ers I con-se-crate to thee, Be pleas'd, most ho-ly Mo-ther, From sin to keep me free.

Words in "Hymns for the Year," No. 217.

---

43. COME, YE LITTLE CHILDREN.

Come, ye lit-tle chil-dren, Un-to me draw nigh; For 'tis such as you That dwell with me on high:

COME, YE LITTLE CHILDREN.

Who in truth and meekness, From all malice free,
Ever serve and love me In simplicity.

Words in "Hymns for the Year," No. 198.

---

44. HEART OF THE HOLY CHILD.

Heart of the Holy Child, Hide me in Thee;
Purest and undefil'd, Purify me!
Joy of my infant life, Far from evil passions rife,
Troubling this world of strife, Keep me with Thee!

Words in "Hymns for the Year," No. 238.

45. O PARADISE.
J. F. BARNETT.

46. O PARADISE.
Harmonised by F. WESTLAKE.

O PARADISE!

1 O PARADISE! O Paradise!
   Who doth not crave for rest?
Who would not seek the happy land
   Where they that loved are blest?
Where loyal hearts and true
   Stand ever in the light,
All rapture through and through,
   In God's most holy sight.

2 O Paradise! O Paradise!
   The world is growing old;
Who would not be at rest and free
   Where love is never cold?
      Where, &c.

3 O Paradise! O Paradise!
   Wherefore doth death delay—
Bright death, that is the welcome dawn
   Of our eternal day?
      Where, &c.

4 O Paradise! O Paradise!
   'Tis weary waiting here:
I long to be where Jesus is,
   To feel, to see Him near.
      Where, &c.

5 O Paradise! O Paradise!
   I want to sin no more;
I want to be as pure on earth
   As on thy spotless shore.
      Where, &c.

6 O Paradise! O Paradise!
   I greatly long to see
The special place my dearest Lord
   Has destined long for me.
      Where, &c.

7 O Paradise! O Paradise!
   I feel 'twill not be long:
Patience! I almost think I hear
   Faint fragments of thy song.
      Where, &c.

47. JESUS, EVER-LOVING SAVIOUR.

Je-sus, e-ver-lov-ing Sa-viour, Thou didst live and die for me;
Liv-ing, I will live to love Thee, Dy-ing, I will die for Thee.
Je-sus! Je-sus! By Thy life and death of sor-row,
Help me in my a-go-ny, Help me in my a-go-ny.

Words in "Hymns for the Year," No. 184.

---

48. THE SNOW LAY ON THE GROUND.
(Roman Christmas Carol.)

The snow lay on the ground, The stars shone bright; When Christ our Lord was born On Christ-mas night, When Christ our Lord was born On Christ-mas night.

CHORUS (ad lib.): Ve-ni-te a-do-re-mus Do-mi-num; Ve-ni-te a-do-re-mus Do-mi-num; Ve-ni-te a-do-re-mus Do-mi-num.

Words in "Hymns for the Year," No. 235.

49. SLEEP OF THE INFANT JESUS.

SLEEP OF THE INFANT JESUS.

(Cradle Song.)

SLUMBER, haste on dewy pinions,
  From thy starry throne descend ;
Gently tow'rd yon little manger
  Let thy golden wand extend.

On His Mother's bosom, slowly,
  Lo ! the Babe reclines His head ;
Sweetly o'er His wearied senses
  Balmy sleep its charm hath spread.

Hark ! the angry blast of winter
  Dies along the snowy plain ;
Fainter grow the rippling murmurs
  On Judæa's distant main.

Through the pine-grove Cedron calmly
  Pours its waves adown the steep ;
Silence reigns o'er things created
  While their Maker's wrapt in sleep.

Hymns and Sacred Songs.

Part II.

CONTAINING

HYMNS, CHIEFLY IN FOUR VOCAL PARTS,

WITH ORGAN ACCOMPANIMENT
AD LIBITUM.

MY GOD, HOW WONDERFUL THOU ART!

E. SILAS.

MY GOD, HOW WONDERFUL THOU ART!

MY GOD, HOW WONDERFUL THOU ART.

MY GOD, HOW WONDERFUL THOU ART.

HAVE MERCY ON US GOD MOST HIGH.

55. HAVE MERCY ON US, GOD MOST HIGH!

B. Molique.

HAVE MERCY ON US, GOD MOST HIGH!

HAVE MERCY ON US, GOD MOST HIGH!

PRAISE WE OUR GOD WITH JOY.

57.   O GOD OF LOVELINESS!

A. S. HOLLOWAY, MUS. DOC.

O GOD OF LOVELINESS

BLEST THREE IN ONE.

The following Hymns may be sung to the same music:—

LORD OF ETERNAL TRUTH.

LORD of eternal truth and might,
  Ruler of nature's changing scheme!
Who dost bring forth the morning light,
  And temper noon's effulgent beam.

Quench Thou in us the flames of strife,
  And bid the heat of passion cease,
From perils guard our feeble life,
  And keep our souls in perfect peace.

Father of mercies! hear our cry!
  Hear us, O sole-begotten Son;
Who with the Holy Ghost most high,
  Reignest while endless ages run.

O THOU TRUE LIFE.

O Thou true life of all that live,
  Who dost, unmov'd, all motion sway;
Who dost the morn and evening give,
  And through its changes guide the day.

Thy light upon our evening pour,
  So may our souls no sunset see,
But death to us an open door
  To an eternal morning be.

Father of mercies! hear our cry;
  Hear us, O sole begotten Son!
Who, with the Holy Ghost most high,
  Reignest while endless ages run.

MAJESTY DIVINE.

HOLY GODHEAD.

HOLY GODHEAD.

61. JESUS IS GOD!

JOHN FRANCIS BARNETT.

JESUS IS GOD:

O JESU! KING MOST WONDERFUL.

62A. MY GOD, O GOODNESS INFINITE.

(The same music as the foregoing, but in the key of F.)

1. My God, O Goodness infinite, My life's true Life art Thou; Lord
2. While night and day my foes allure, In Thee do I confide; Take

of my heart, my spouse most sweet, My love to Thee I vow. Je-
Thou and place my heart secure, Within Thy piercèd side. With

sus, for Thee I pine away, My love and my desire; And,
Thy sweet chains, O Jesus, bind My rebel heart to Thee; Till

[For last verse.]

more enamour'd day by day, I burn with heav'nly fire.
death, my safety I will find In such captivity. A-men.

64. CROWN HIM, THE VIRGIN'S SON.

2.
Crown Him, the Lord of Love;
Behold His hands and side,—
Rich wounds, still visible above
In beauty glorified:
No angel in the sky
Can fully bear that sight,
But downward bends his burning eye
At mysteries so bright.

3.
Crown Him, the Lord of Peace,
Whose power a sceptre sways
From pole to pole, that wars may cease,
Absorb'd in prayer and praise:
His reign shall know no end,
And round His piercèd feet
Fair flowers of Paradise extend
Their fragrance ever sweet.

No. **66**, *Accompaniment*, see No. 102.

67. CREATOR OF THE STARRY FRAME.

68. HARK! AN AWFUL VOICE IS SOUNDING.

HARK! AN AWFUL VOICE IS SOUNDING.

JESU, CREATOR OF THE WORLD.

FREDERICK WESTLAKE.

For this Thy sacred heart was pierced,
And both with blood and water ran;
To cleanse us from the stains of guilt,
And be the hope and strength of man.

To God the Father and the Son
All praise, and power, and glory be
With Thee, O holy Paraclete,
Henceforth through all eternity.
Amen.

The following Hymn may be sung to the same music.

CREATOR OF THE STARRY FRAME.

CREATOR of the starry frame,
Eternal light of all who live!
Jesu, Redeemer of mankind!
An ear to Thy poor suppliants give.

When man, o'erwhelm'd in sin and death,
Was wholly lost in Satan's snare,
Love brought Thee down to cure our ills,
By taking of those ills a share.

Thy love for guilty men it was
That caused Thy sacred blood to flow
When issuing from Thy virgin shrine,
Thou didst to death a victim go.

Great Judge of all, in that last day,
When friends shall fail and foes combine,
Look down in pity then, we pray,
And guard us with thine arm divine.

JESU, CREATOR OF THE WORLD.
(FOR FOUR VOICES.)

70. O JESU, THOU THE BEAUTY ART.

E. Silas.

1. O Jesu, Thou the beauty art Of angel worlds above; Thy Name is music to the heart, Enchanting it with love. Celestial sweetness unalloy'd, Who eat Thee hunger still; Who drink of Thee still feel a void, Which nought but Thou canst fill. Amen.

2. O loving Jesu, hear the sighs Which unto Thee I send; To Thee mine inmost spirit cries, My being's hope and end. Stay with us, Lord, and with Thy light Illume the soul's abyss; Dispel the darkness of our night, And fill the world with bliss. Amen.

The following may also be used—

JESU, MY SOUL HATH IN THY LOVE.

1.

Jesu, my soul hath in Thy love
A food that never cloys;
A sacred foretaste from above
Of Paradisal joys.
Thrice happy he, who loving Thee,
Doth Thy true sweetness know;
All else becomes but vanity
Thenceforth to him below.

2.

O fairest of the sons of day!
More fragrant than the rose!
O brighter than the dazzling ray
That in the sunbeam glows!
O Thou whose love alone is all
That mortal can desire!
Whose image doth my heart enthrall,
And with delight inspire.

COME ALL YE FAITHFUL.

72. DEAR LITTLE ONE HOW SWEET THOU ART.
(CHRISTMAS CRADLE-SONG.)
Giulio Roberti.

DEAR LITTLE ONE HOW SWEET THOU ART.

* This may be sung either in Unison, or as a Duett, Trio, or Quartett.

O LOVELY VOICES OF THE SKY.

74. NONE OF ALL THE NOBLEST CITIES.

NONE OF ALL THE NOBLEST CITIES.

O SION, OPEN WIDE THE GATES.

The following Hymn may be sung to the same music:

IT is my sweetest comfort, Lord,
 And will for ever be,
To muse upon the gracious truth
 Of Thy humanity.
O joy, there sitteth in our flesh,
 Upon a throne of light,
One of a human Mother born,
 In blazing Godhead bright.

Though earth's foundations should be **moved**
 Down to their lowest deep;
Though all the trembling universe
 Into destruction sweep;
For ever God, for ever man,
 My Jesus shall endure;
And fix'd on Him, my hope remains
 Eternally secure.

76. O'ERWHELMED IN DEPTHS OF WOE.

G. A. MACFARREN.

O'ERWHELMED IN DEPTHS OF WOE.

77.
HAIL! WOUNDS WHICH THROUGH ETERNAL YEARS.

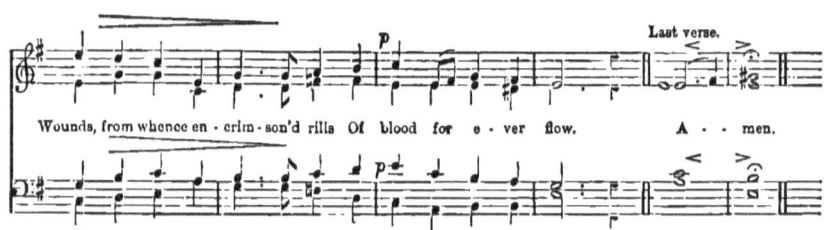

How doth th' ensanguined thorny crown
   That beauteous brow transpierce!
How do the nails those hands and feet
   Contract with tortures fierce!

He bows His head, and forth at last
   His loving spirit soars;
Yet, even after death, His heart
   For us its tribute pours.

Oh, come all ye in whom are fix'd
   The deadly stains of sin,
Come, wash in this all-saving Blood,
   And ye shall be made clean.

Praise Him, who with the Father sits
   Enthroned upon the skies;
Whose Blood redeems our souls from guilt,
   Whose Spirit sanctifies.

The following Hymn may be sung to the same music:—

FROM circlets starr'd with many a gem,
   And set in rich array;
I turn me to a Diadem—
   More precious far than they.

Dread Crown of Thorns! which Jesus wore,
   Pledge of His dying love!
When clouds arise and tempests roar,
   Shine on me from above.

Oh, let the points that pierced His Brow
   Transpierce this faithless breast;
That thought, and will, and wish, and vow,
   In Christ may ever rest!

O Wreath of agony untold,
   With woe on ev'ry spine!
The hearts of weeping sinners hold,
   And heal and soften mine.

78. JESU TO THEE WE LOOK

The following Hymn may be sung to the same music.

O YE who seek the Lord,
  Lift up your eyes on high,
For thence He doth the sign accord
  Of His bright Majesty
We see a dazzling Light
  That shall outlive all time,
More ancient far than depth or height,
  Limitless and sublime.

'Tis He for Israel's fold
  And heathen tribes decreed;
The King to Abra'm pledged of old,
  And his unfailing seed.
Prophets foretold His birth,
  And witnessed when He came;
The Father speaks to all the earth,
  To hear and own His name.

O JESU! OUR REDEMPTION.

ALL YE WHO SEEK A SURE RELIEF.

ALL YE WHO SEEK A SURE RELIEF.

82. TO CHRIST THE PRINCE OF PEACE.

JULES BENEDICT.

TO CHRIST THE PRINCE OF PEACE.

* The Accompaniment may here be omitted until ¶

TO CHRIST THE PRINCE OF PEACE.

N.B.—The entire Hymn may be sung, if preferred, in either of the three ways above given.

GOD OF MERCY AND COMPASSION.

GOD OF MERCY AND COMPASSION.

ACCOMPANIMENT IN THE FORM OF A COMPRESSED SCORE.

84. SOUL OF JESUS, MAKE ME HOLY.

FREDERICK WESTLAKE.

1. Soul of Jesus, make me holy, Make me contrite, meek, and lowly;
2. Save me, Body of my Lord, Save a sinner vile, abhorred;

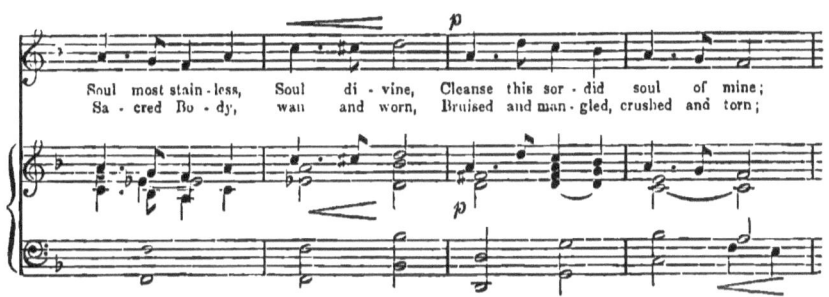

Soul most stainless, Soul divine, Cleanse this sordid soul of mine;
Sacred Body, wan and worn, Bruised and mangled, crushed and torn;

Hallow this polluted soul, Purify it, make it whole;
Pierced hands, and feet, and side; Scourg'd, insulted, crucified;

SOUL OF JESUS, MAKE ME HOLY.

Soul of Jesus, hal-low me;
Save me, to the cross I flee;
} Mi - se - re - re Do - mi - ne!

[*N.B.*—*The following (or more) verses of the hymn may be sung to the music as above, or the last stanza may follow at once.*]

3.

Blood of Jesus, Stream of life,
Sacred stream with blessing rife,
From thy broken Body shed,
On the cross, that Altar dread ;
Blood most precious, Fount divine,
Fill my heart and make it thine ;
Blood of Christ my cleansing be ;
   Miserere Domine !

4.

Jesus, by the wondrous power
Of thine awful Passion hour,
By the unimagined woe
Mortal man may never know,
By the cross upon Thee laid,
By the ransom Thou hast paid,
By thy passion comfort me ;
   Miserere Domine !

[*Last Stanza.*]

Mi - se - re - re! let me be Ne - ver part-ed, Lord, from Thee;

Guard me from my ruth-less foe; Save me from e - ter - nal woe. In the dread - ful

SOUL OF JESUS, MAKE ME HOLY

The following Hymn may be sung to the same music.

Jesu! as though Thyself wert here,
I draw in trembling sorrow near,
And hanging o'er Thy form divine,
Kneel down to kiss these wounds of Thine.

Oh, by those sacred hands and feet,
For me so mangled, I entreat
My Saviour turn me not away,
But let me here for ever stay.

Hail, awful brow! Hail, thorny wreath!
Hail, countenance now pale in death,
Whose glance but late so brightly blazed
That angels trembled as they gazed.

86. THOU LOVING MAKER OF MANKIND.

87. O, SOUL OF JESUS, SICK TO DEATH.

O, SOUL OF JESUS, SICK TO DEATH.

CHRIST THE LORD IS RISEN TO-DAY.

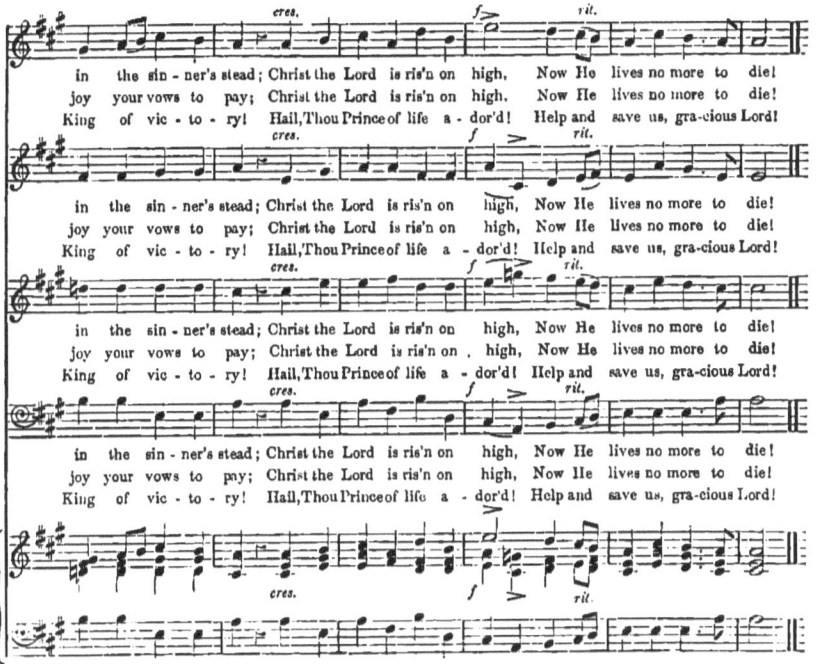

The following Hymn may be sung to the same music:

By the first bright Easter-day,
When the stone was roll'd away;
By the glory round Thee shed
At Thy rising from the dead;
  King of glory, hear our cry;
    Make us soon Thy joys to see,
  Where enthron'd in majesty
    Countless angels sing to Thee.

By Thy parting blessing giv'n
As Thou didst ascend to heav'n
By the cloud of living light
That receiv'd Thee out of sight;
  King of glory, hear our cry;
    Make us soon Thy joys to see,
  Where enthron'd in majesty
    Countless angels sing to Thee.

By that rushing sound of might
Coming down from heaven's height;
By the cloven tongue of fire,
Holy Ghost, our hearts inspire.
  King of glory, hear our cry;
    Make us soon Thy joys to see,
  Where enthron'd in majesty
    Countless angels sing to Thee.

88a. CHRIST THE LORD IS RISEN TO-DAY.

J. R. SCHACHNER.

CHRIST THE LORD IS RISEN TO-DAY.

3.

Say, O wond'ring Mary, say,
What thou sawest on thy way.
"I beheld, where Christ had lain,
Empty tomb and angels twain ;
I beheld the glory bright
Of the rising Lord of light :
Christ my hope is ris'n again ;
Now He lives, and lives to reign."

4.

Christ, who once for sinners bled,
Now the first-born from the dead,
Thron'd in endless might and power,
Lives and reigns for evermore.
Hail, eternal hope on high ;
Hail, thou King of victory ;
Hail, thou Prince of life ador'd :
Help and save us, gracious Lord.

Nam'd of old High-Priest for ever,
  By the Father's stedfast oath,
Rise, O Advocate Almighty!
  Rise, O Priest and Victim both;
Swiftly speed thy glorious way
Back to golden realms of day.

Lo, tis done! O'er death victorious,
  Christ ascends His starry throne;
There from all His labours resting
  Still He travails for His own;
Still our fate His Heart employs
Ev'n amid eternal joys.

90. NOW AT THE LAMB'S HIGH ROYAL FEAST.

Last time.

For the hymn, "Wave the Sweet Censer," the ending will be as follows:—

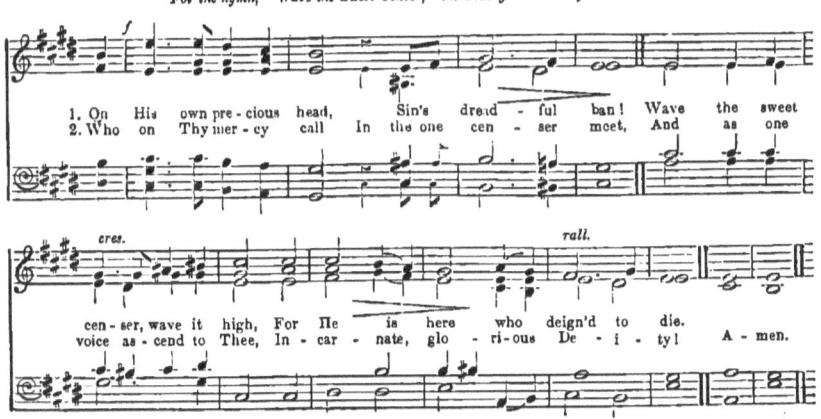

WAVE THE SWEET CENSER.

1.
Wave the sweet censer,—wave
To Him who came to save
 The soul of man;
* Enduring in our stead,
 On His own precious head,
 Sin's dreadful ban!
Wave the sweet censer,—wave it high,
For He is here who deign'd to die!

2.
Lord! let the mystic cloud
Thine Holy Altar shroud
 In fragrance sweet;
* And may the prayer of all
 Who on Thy mercy call
 In the one censer meet,
And as one voice ascend to Thee,
Incarnate, glorious Deity! Amen.

* The music repeats these lines.

92. O THOU ETERNAL KING MOST HIGH.

GERMAN MELODY.

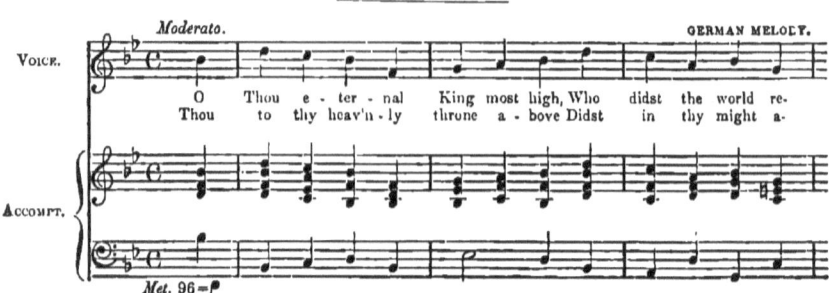

O Thou e-ter-nal King most high, Who didst the world re-deem; And conquering death and hell, re-ceive A dig-ni-ty su-preme:
Thou to thy heav'n-ly throne a-bove Didst in thy might a-scend; Thence-forth to reign in sov-reign pow'r, And glo-ry with-out end.

There, seated in thy majesty,
  To Thee submissive bow
The spacious earth, the highest heaven,
  The depths of hell below.

There, waiting for thy faithful souls,
  Be Thou to us, O Lord,
Our peerless joy while here we stay,
  In Heav'n our great reward.

Renew our strength,—our sins forgive;
  Our miseries efface;
And lift our souls aloft to Thee,
  By thy celestial grace.

So, when Thou shinest on the clouds,
  With thy angelic train,
May we be sav'd from vengeance due,
  And our lost crowns regain.

The following Hymn may be sung to the same music.

O THOU, IN WHOM MY LOVE DOTH FIND.

O Thou, in whom my love doth find
  Its rest and perfect end;
O Jesu, Saviour of mankind,
  And their eternal friend!

Return, return, pure Light of Light,
  To thy dread throne again;
Go forth victorious from the fight,
  And in thy glory reign.

Ye Heav'ns, your gates eternal raise,
  Come forth to meet your King;
Come forth with joy, and sing his praise,—
  His praise eternal sing!

O Fount of mercy! Light of Heaven!
  Our darkness cast away;
And grant us all, through Thee forgiven,
  To see the perfect day.

93. O THOU, IN WHOM OUR LOVE DOTH FIND.

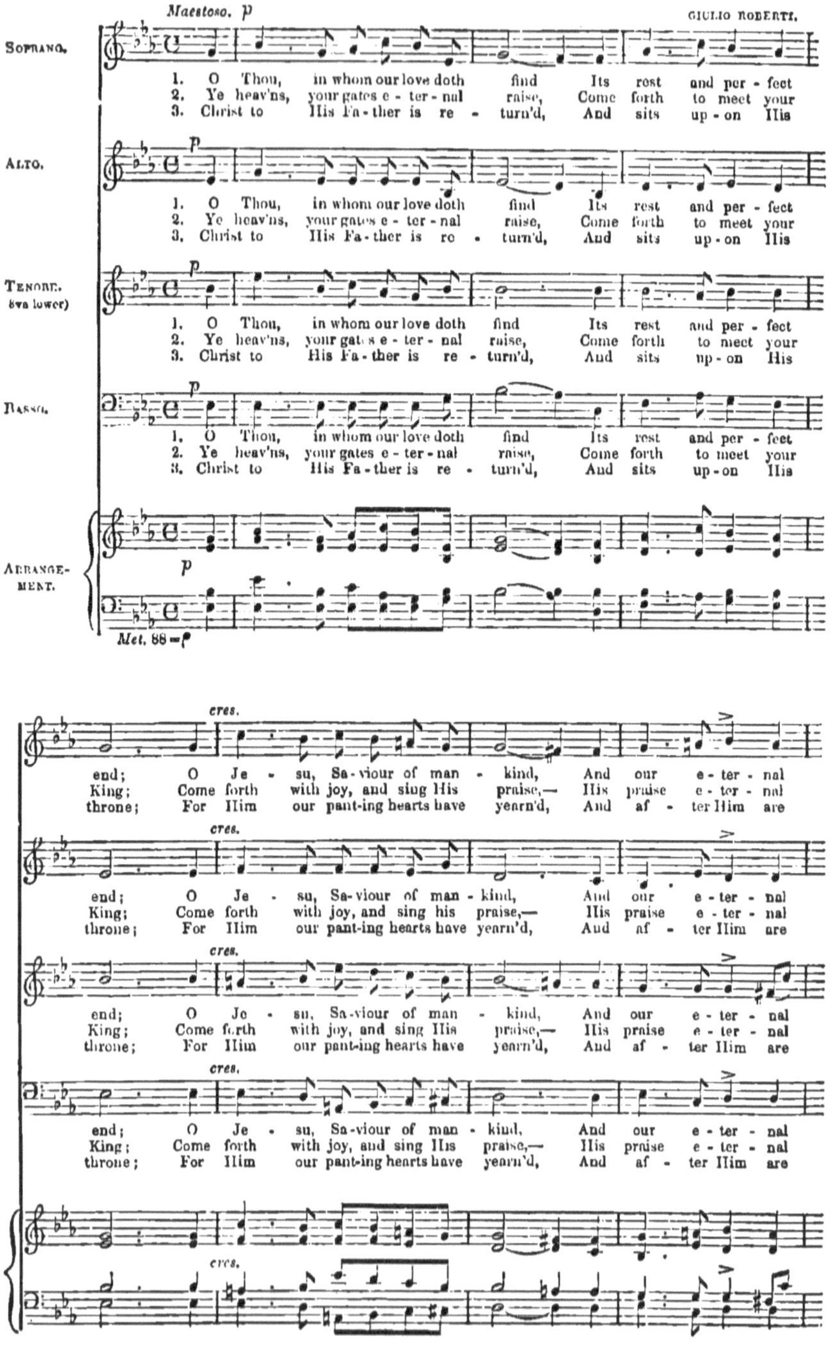

GIULIO ROBERTI.

COME, HOLY GHOST.

J. Richardson.

Met. 96 = ♩

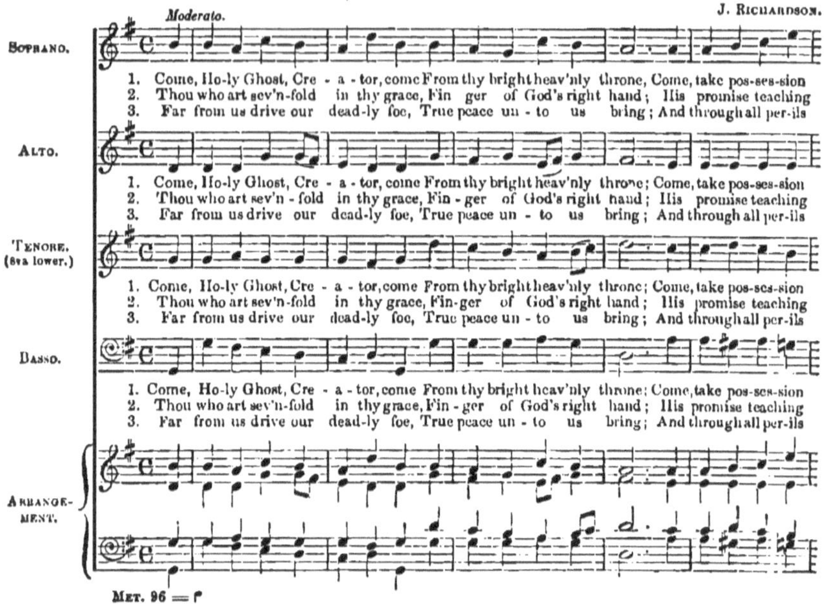

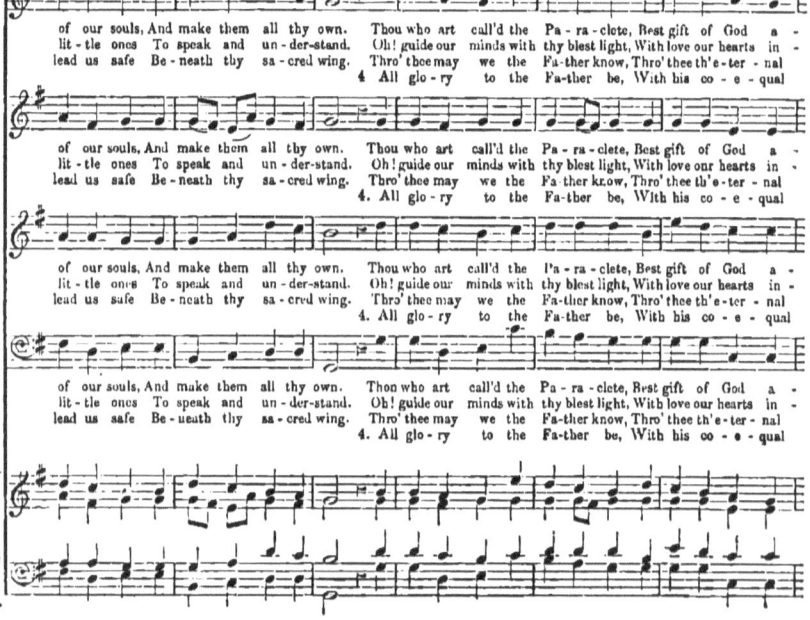

COME, HOLY GHOST.

The following Hymn may be sung to the same music:

Again the slowly circling year
   Brings round the blessed hour,
When on the Church the Comforter
   Came down in grace and power.

God of all grace, to Thee we pray,
   To Thee adoring bend,
Into our hearts this sacred day
   Thy Spirit's fulness send.

Thou who in ages past didst pour
   Thy graces from above,
Thy grace in us where lost restore,
   And 'stablish peace and love.

All glory to the Father be,
   And to the Son who rose,
Glory, O Holy Ghost, to Thee,
   While age on ages flows.

No. 95, *Accompaniment, see* No. 124.

96. COME, O CREATOR SPIRIT BLEST.

W. M. Lutz.

Come, O Cre - a - tor Spi - rit blest, And in our souls take up Thy rest; Come with Thy grace and heav'n - ly aid, To fill the hearts which Thou hast made. A - - - men.

2.

Great Paraclete, to Thee we cry,
O highest gift of God most high,
O Fount of life, O fire of love,
And sweet anointing from above.

3.

Thou in Thy sevenfold gifts art known;
The finger of God's hand we own;
The promise of the Father Thou,
Who dost the tongue with pow'r endow.

4.

Our senses kindle from above,
And make our hearts o'erflow with love;
With patience firm and virtue high
The weakness of our flesh supply.

5.

Drive far from us the foe we dread,
And grant us Thy true peace instead;
So shall we not, with Thee for guide,
Turn from the path of life aside.

6.

Oh, may Thy grace on us bestow
The Father and the Son to know,
And Thee through endless times confess'd
Of Both th' eternal Spirit blest.

7.

All glory, while the ages run,
Be to the Father, and the Son
Who rose from death; the same to Thee,
O Holy Ghost, eternally.

97. COME, HOLY GHOST, CREATOR, COME.

COME, HOLY GHOST, CREATOR, COME.

N.B. If desired, this page may be used as a single stanza melody.

98. COME, HOLY GHOST, SEND DOWN THOSE BEAMS.

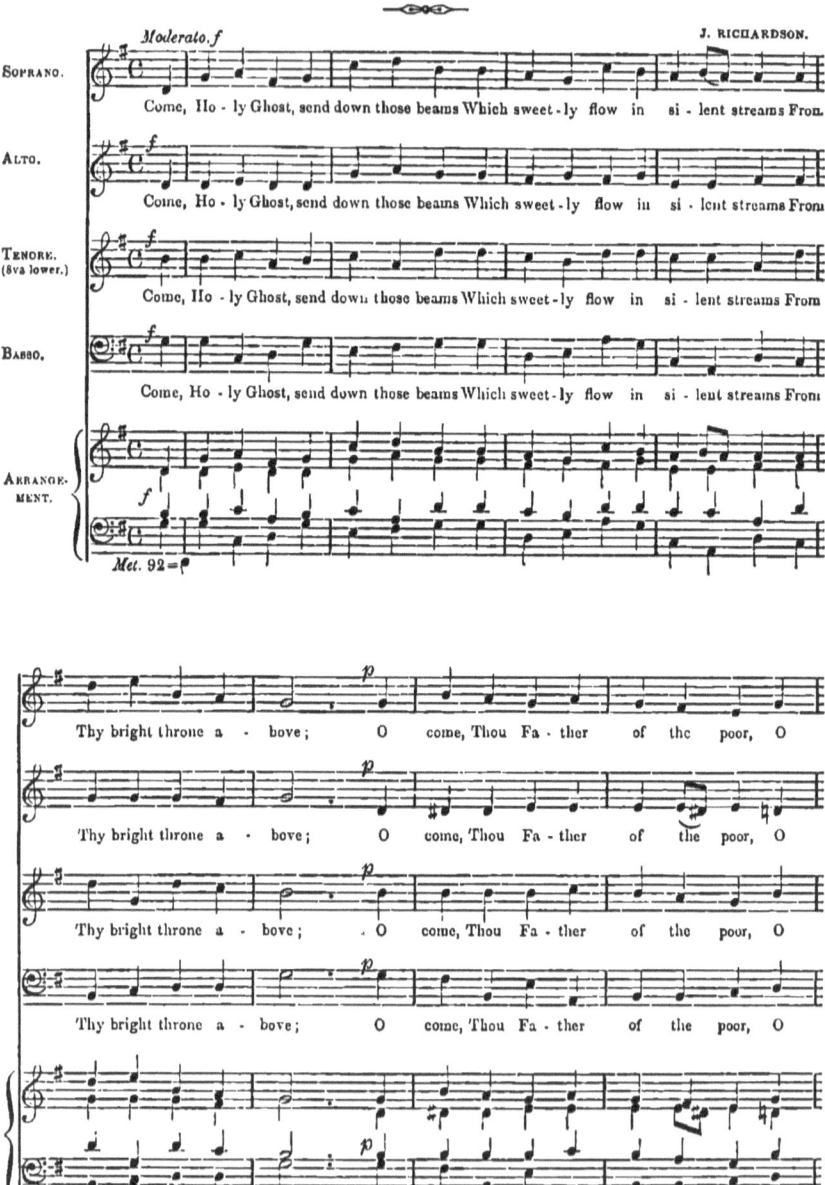

COME, HOLY GHOST, SEND DOWN THOSE BEAMS.

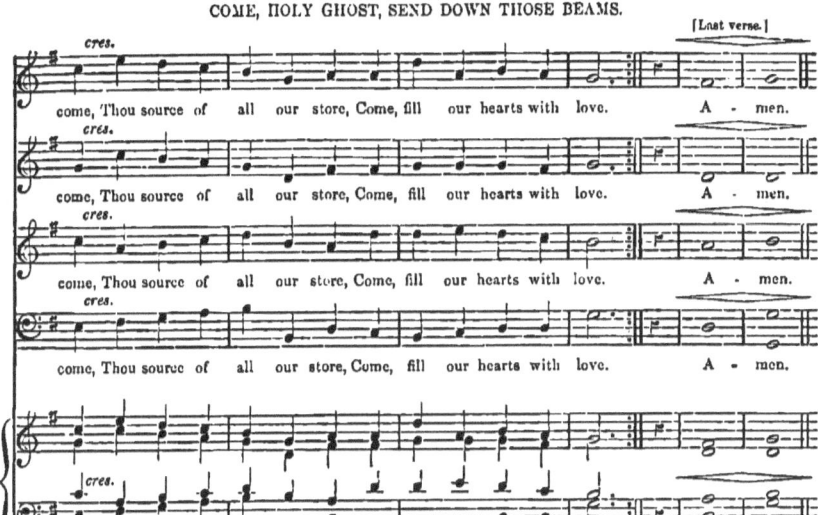

O Thou, of comforters the best,
O Thou, the soul's delightful guest,
 The pilgrim's sweet relief;
Thou art true rest in toil and sweat,
Refreshment in th' excess of heat,
 And solace in our grief.

Thrice-blessed Light, shoot home Thy darts,
And pierce the centres of those hearts
 Whose faith aspires to Thee;
Without Thy Godhead nothing can
Have any price or worth in man,
 Nothing can harmless be.

Lord, wash our sinful stains away,
Refresh from Heaven our barren clay,
 Our wounds and bruises heal;
To thy sweet yoke our stiff necks bow,
Warm with Thy fire our hearts of snow,
 Our wandering feet repeal.

Grant to Thy faithful, dearest Lord,
Whose only hope is Thy sure word,
 The seven gifts of Thy Spirit;
Grant us in life Thy helping grace,
Grant us at death to see Thy face,
 And endless joy inherit.

The following Hymn may be sung to the same music.

COME, Holy Ghost, Thy grace inspire.
Who, from the Son as from the Sire,
 Dost equally proceed;
Within our hearts divinely glow,
Our lips with eloquence endow,
 And strengthen us in need.

Thou to the lowly dost display
The beautiful and perfect way
 Of justice and of peace;
Avoiding every stubborn heart,
Thou to the simple dost impart
 True wisdom's rich increase.

Teach us to aim at Heaven's high prize,
And for its glory to despise
 The world and all below:
Cleanse us from sin, direct us right,
Illuminate us with Thy light,
 Thy peace on us bestow.

So unto Thee, who with the Son
And Father art for ever One,
 The Lord of earth and heaven,
Be, through eternal length of days,
All honour, glory, blessing, praise,
 And adoration, given!

No. 99, *Accompaniment,* see No. 65.

O HEAVENLY JERUSALEM.

101. JERUSALEM, THOU CITY BLEST!

JERUSALEM, THOU CITY BLEST!

102. THE JOYS AND GLORIES OF HEAVEN.

There a Paradisal perfume
  Breathes upon the air serene;
There crystalline waters flowing
  Keep the grass for ever green,
And the golden orchards show
Fruits that ne'er corruption know.

There no sun his circuit wheeleth;
  There no moon or stars appear;
Thither night and darkness come not;
  Death hath no dominion there:
In its stead, the Lamb's pure ray
Scatters round eternal day.

There the saints of God resplendent
  As the sun in all his might,
Evermore rejoice together,
  Crown'd with diadems of light,
And from peril safe at last,
Reckon up their triumphs past.

Happy he, who with them seated
  Doth in all their glory share,
O that I, my days completed,
  Might be but admitted there!
There with them the praise to sing
Of my beauteous God and King.

103. LIGHT OF THE ANXIOUS HEART.

MEYER LUTZ.

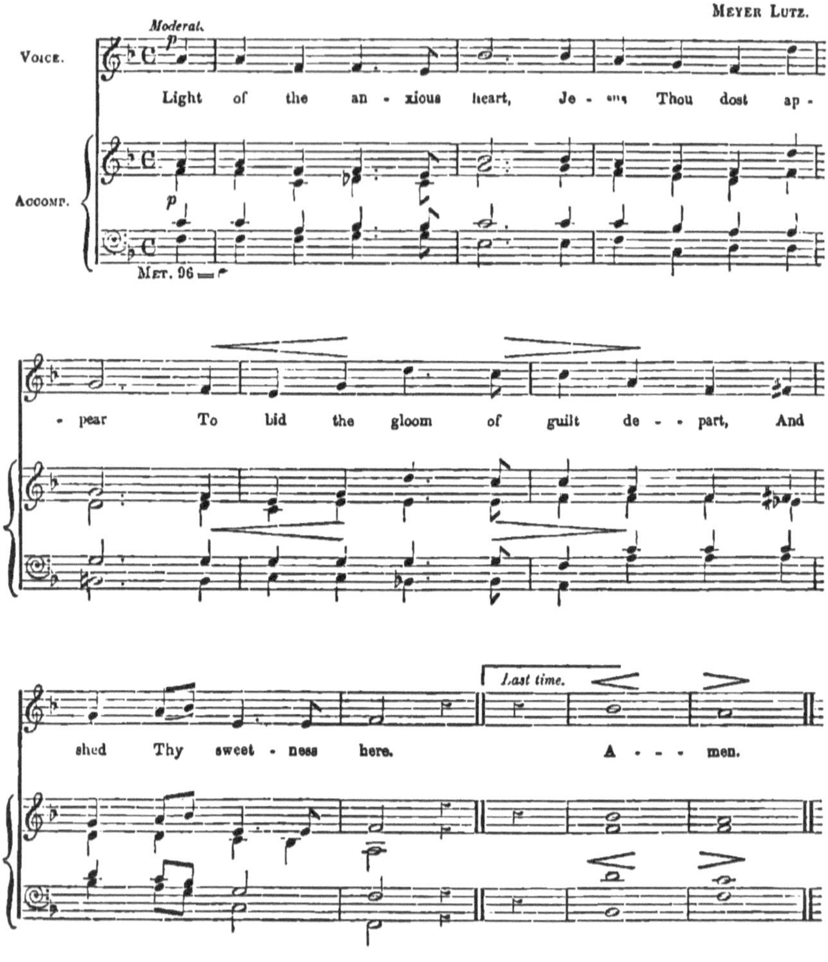
Moderat.
VOICE.
ACCOMP.
MET. 96
Light of the an - xious heart, Je - sus Thou dost ap -
- pear To bid the gloom of guilt de - - part, And
shed Thy sweet - ness here.
Last time.
A - - - men.

Joyous is He with whom,
God's word, Thou dost abide,
Sweet Light of our Eternal home,
To fleshly sense denied.

Brightness of God above
Unfathomable grace,
Thy presence be a fount of love
Within Thy chosen place!

LOVING SHEPHERD OF THY SHEEP.

Thou didst give Thine own life that I might live; May I love Thee day by day, Gladly Thy sweet will obey.
may I go Walking in Thy steps below; Then before Thy Father's throne Jesu claim me for Thine own.

N.B. This Melody differently arranged will be found at No. 84.

The following Hymn may be sung to the same music:

Jesus, Lord, be Thou my own;
Thee I long for, Thee alone;
All myself I give to Thee;
Do whate'er Thou wilt with me.

Life without Thy love would be
Death, O Sovereign Good, to me;
Bound and held by Thy dear chains
Captive now my heart remains.

Thou, O God, my heart inflame,
Give that love which Thou dost claim;
Payment I will ask for none;
Love demands but love alone.

God of beauty, Lord of light,
Thy good will is my delight;
Now henceforth Thy will divine
Ever shall in all be mine.

105. O JESU, JOY OF LOVING HEARTS!

O JESU, JOY OF LOVING HEARTS!

No. 106, *Accompaniment*, see No. 100.

107. JESUS THE VERY THOUGHT OF THEE.

G. H. TILBURY.

JESUS THE VERY THOUGHT OF THEE.

'TIS THY GOOD PLEASURE.

In Thee all pure affections live,
To love Thou dost perfection give;
While ever burning with desires
The loving soul to Thee aspires.
          O will of God, &c.

Thou makest crosses soft and light,
And death itself seem sweet and bright:
No cross nor fear that soul dismays
Whose will to Thee united stays.
          O will of God! O will Divine!
          All, all our love be ever Thine.

To Thee I consecrate and give
My heart and being while I live;
Jesus, Thy heart alone shall be
My love for all eternity.
          O will of God, &c.

Alike in pleasure and in pain
To please me is my joy and gain;
That, O my Love, which pleases Thee
Shall evermore seem best to me.
          May heaven and earth with love fulfil,
          My God, Thy ever-blessed will!

No. 111, *Accompaniment*, see No. 69. — No. 112, *Accompaniment*, see No. 53.

113. MY LORD, MY GOD, WHAT WILLEST THOU?

Meyer Lutz.

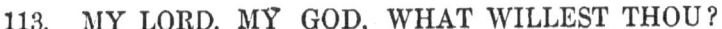

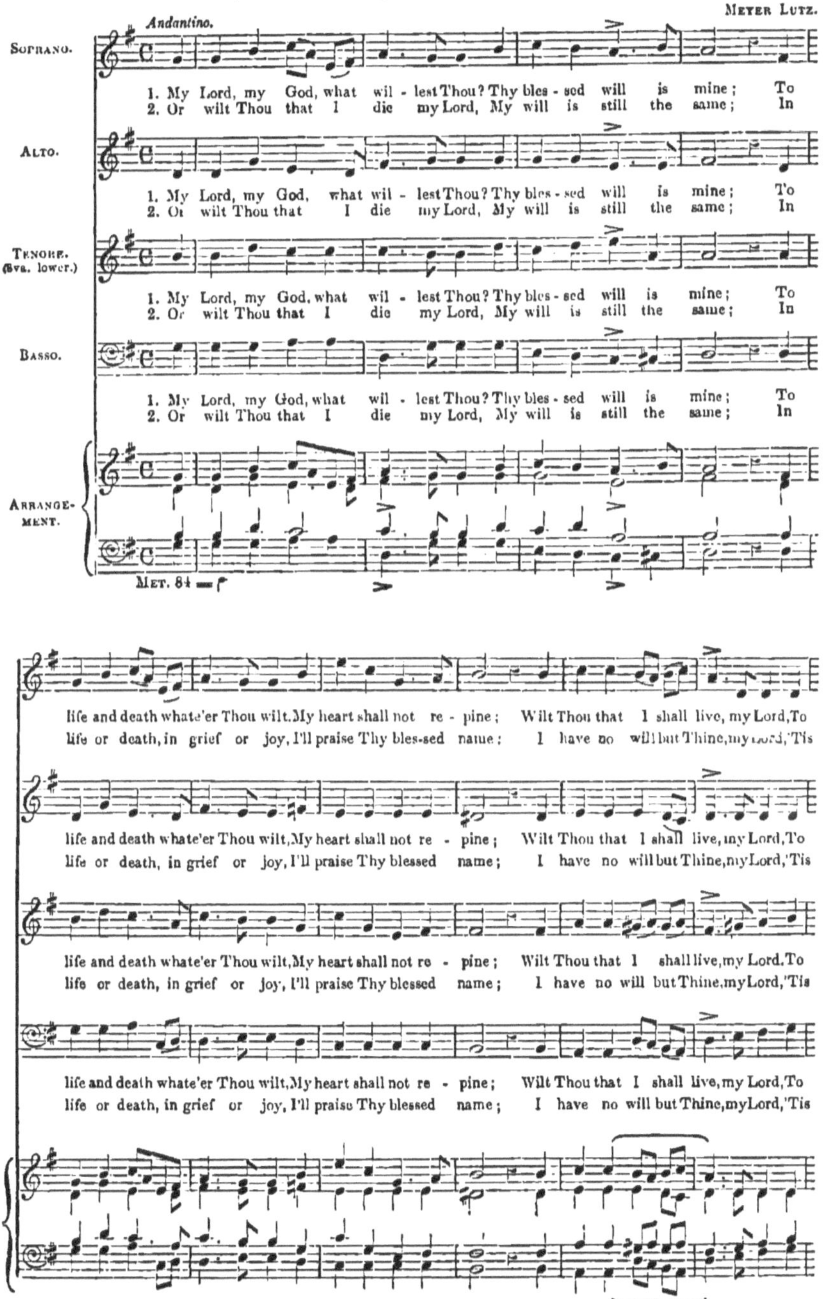

MY LORD, MY GOD, WHAT WILLEST THOU?

The following Hymn may be sung to the same music:

> In Christ's dear Name with courage bear
>   Whatever ills betide;
> For worldly good is oft a snare,
>   And fills the heart with pride.
> What seems a loss will often prove
>   To be our truest gain;
> And pains endured with patient love
>   A jewelled crown obtain.
>
> Brief is this life, and brief its pain,
>   But long the bliss to come;
> And trials borne for Christ attain
>   A place with martyrdom.
> The Christian soul by patience grows
>   More perfect day by day,
> And brighter still and brighter glows
>   With Heaven's eternal ray.

MY GOD, O GOODNESS INFINITE.

The following Hymn may be sung to the same music:

THE shadows of the evening hours
    Fall from the dark'ning sky;
Upon the fragrance of the flowers
    The dews of evening lie:
Before Thy throne, O Lord of Heaven,
    We kneel at close of day;
Look on Thy children from on high,
    And hear us while we pray.

The sorrows of Thy servants, Lord,
    O do not Thou despise;
But let the incense of our prayers
    Before Thy mercy rise.
The brightness of the coming night
    Upon the darkness rolls;
With hopes of future glory chase
    The shadows on our souls.

    Let peace, O Lord, Thy peace, O God
        Upon our souls descend;
    From midnight fears and perils Thou
        Our trembling hearts defend.
    Give us a respite from our toil;
        Calm and subdue our woes;
    Through the long day we suffer, Lord,
        O give us now repose.

115. MY SHEPHERD IS THE LIVING GOD.

* This music may be used for a stanza of four lines by omitting the eight bars between the asterisks.

MY SHEPHERD IS THE LIVING GOD.

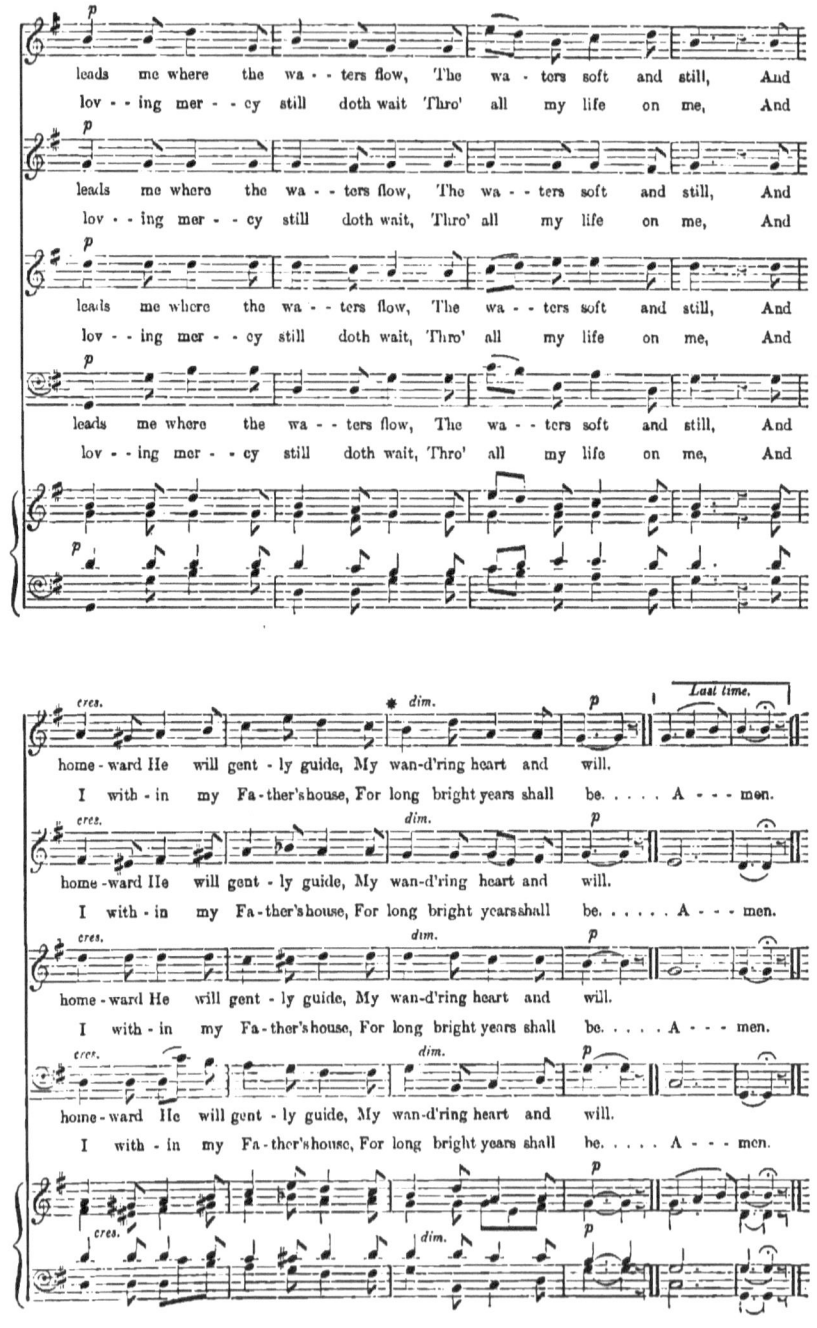

116. I LOVE THEE, O THOU LORD MOST HIGH.

May memory no thought suggest,
But shall to Thy pure glory tend,
My understanding find no rest
Except in Thee, its only end.

My God, I here protest to Thee,
No other will I have than thine,
Whatever Thou hast giv'n to me,
I here again to Thee resign.

All mine is Thine,—say but the word,
Whate'er Thou willest shall be done;
I know Thy love, all-gracious Lord,
I know it seeks my good alone.

Apart from Thee all things are nought,
Then grant, O my supremest bliss,
Grant me to love Thee as I ought,
Thou givest all in giving this!

117. O JESU! THOU THE BEAUTY ART.

WILHELM SCHULTHES.

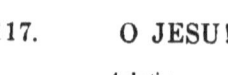

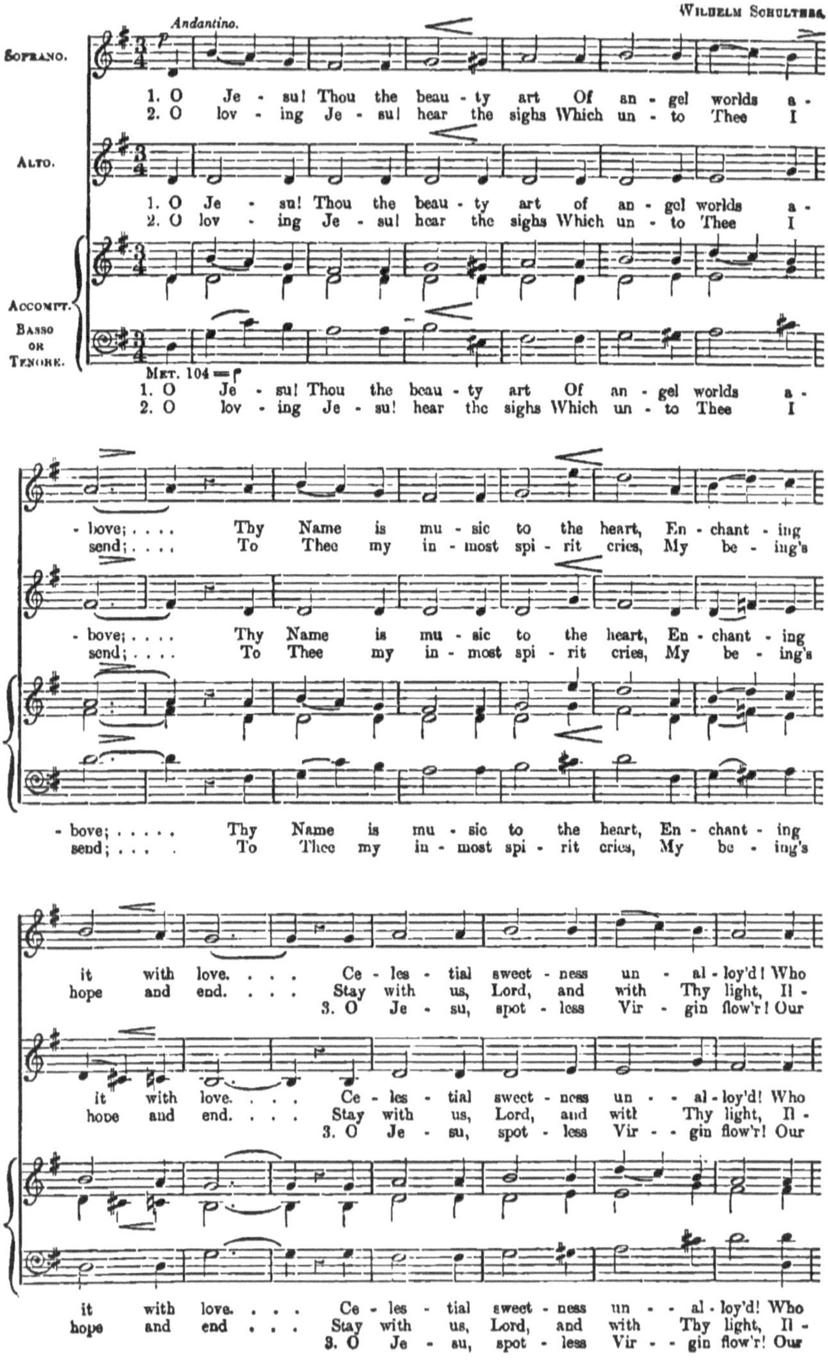
Andantino.
SOPRANO.
ALTO.
ACCOMPT.
BASSO OR TENORE.
MET. 104 =
1. O Je - su! Thou the beau - ty art Of an - gel worlds a -
2. O lov - ing Je - su! hear the sighs Which un - to Thee I
- bove; . . . . Thy Name is mu - sic to the heart, En - chant - ing
send; . . . . To Thee my in - most spi - rit cries, My be - ing's
it with love. . . . Ce - les - tial sweet - ness un - al - loy'd! Who
hope and end. . . . Stay with us, Lord, and with Thy light, Il -
3. O Je - su, spot - less Vir - gin flow'r! Our

O JESU! THOU THE BEAUTY ART.

118. HOW GENTLY FLOW THE SILENT YEARS.

JOHN FRANCIS BARNETT

HOW GENTLY FLOW THE SILENT YEARS.

The following Hymn may be sung to the same music:

I DWELL a captive in this Heart,
    Inflamed with love divine;
'Tis here I live alone in peace,
    And constant joy is mine.
It is the Heart of God's own Son
    In His humanity,
Who, all enamour'd of my soul,
    Here burns with love of me.

Here like the dove within the ark
    Securely I repose;
Since now the Lord is my defence,
    I fear no earthly foes.
What though I suffer, still in love
    I ever true will be;
My love of God shall deeper grow
    When crosses fall on me.

From every bond of earth, O Lord,
    Thy grace hath set me free;
My soul deliver'd from the snare
    Enjoys true liberty.
Nought more can I desire than this,
    To see Thy face in Heaven;
And this I hope since He on earth
    His Heart in pledge hath given.

119. THEY WHOM WE LOVED ON EARTH.

THEY WHOM WE LOVED ON EARTH.

THEY WHOM WE LOVED ON EARTH.

120 & 121. OH! WHY ART THOU SORROWFUL.

OH! WHY ART THOU SORROWFUL.

OH! WHY ART THOU SORROWFUL.

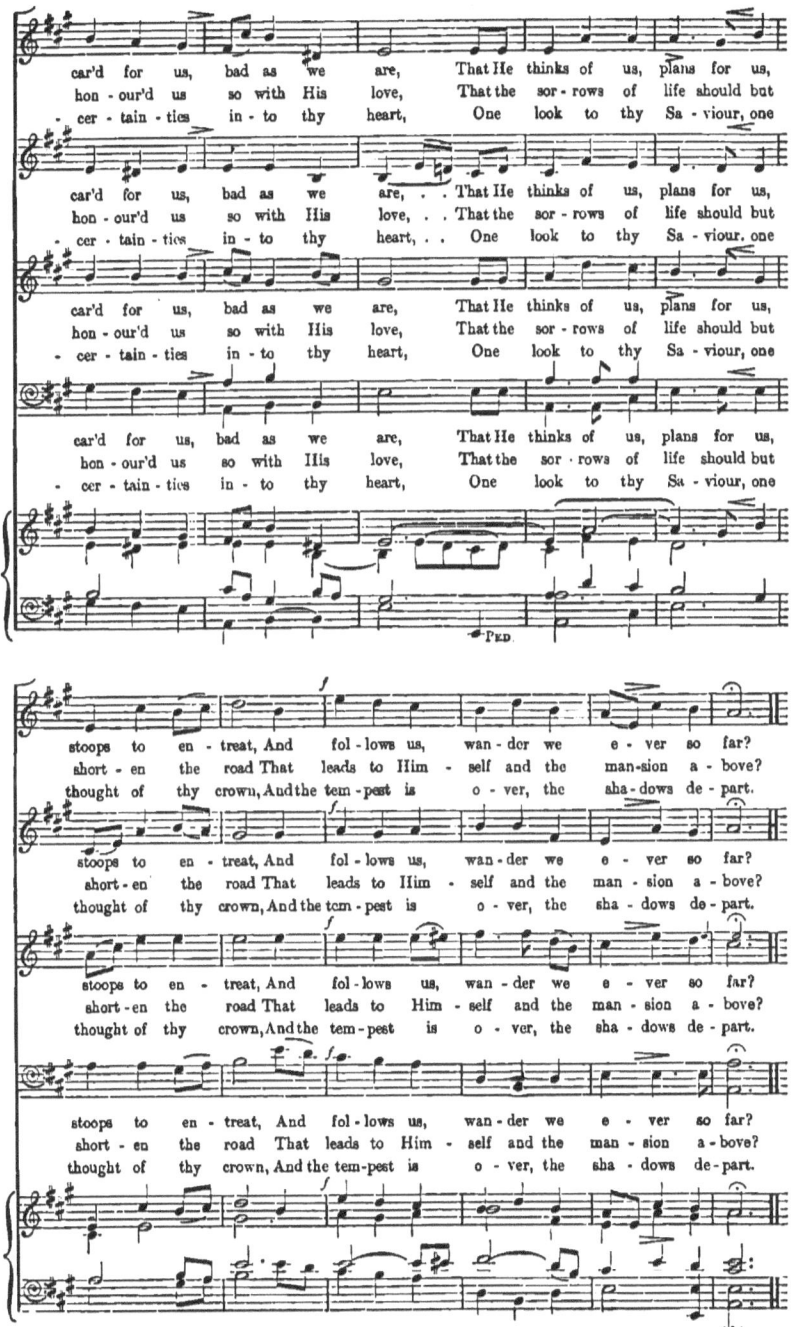

122. CHRISTIAN SOUL, DOST THOU DESIRE?

The following hymn may be sung to the same music:—

Jesus, Lord, be Thou my own;
Thee I long for,—Thee alone!
All myself I give to Thee,
Do whate'er Thou wilt with me.

Life, without Thy love, would be,
Death, O Sovereign Good! to me.
Bound and held by Thy dear chains
Captive now my heart remains.

Thou, O God, my heart inflame,
Give that love which Thou dost claim,
Payment I will ask for none,
Love demands but love alone.

God of beauty, Lord of light
Thy good will is my delight;
Now henceforth, Thy will divine,
Ever shall in all be Thine.

123. THY HOME IS WITH THE HUMBLE, LORD.

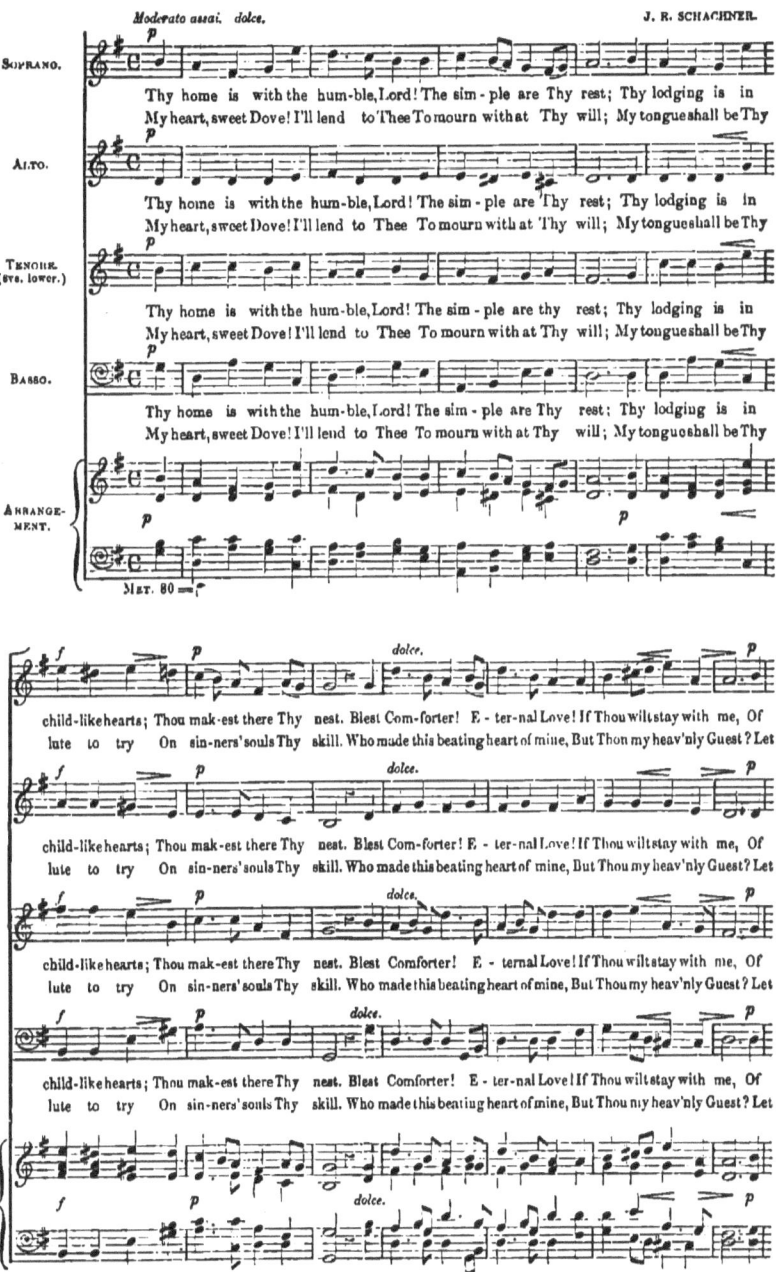

THY HOME IS WITH THE HUMBLE, LORD.

The following hymn may be sung to the same music:—

I worship Thee, sweet will of God!
And all Thy ways adore,
And every day I live I seem
To love Thee more and more.
I love to kiss each print where thou
Hast set Thine unseen feet;
I cannot fear, O blessed Will!
Thine empire is so sweet.

I have no cares, O blessed Will!
For all my cares are Thine;
I live in triumph, Lord! for Thou
Hast made Thy triumphs mine.
And when it seems no chance or change
From grief can set me free,
Hope finds its strength in helplessness,
And waits with joy on Thee.

Then from My lips that sweet inviting word
That bids thee love Me shall by thee be heard,
How much I always loved thee thou shalt see,
And how ungrateful thou hast been to Me.

Sweet contrite tears thy wounds of sin shall heal,
The ardour of My love thou then shalt feel,
And here I wait thee to bestow in love
A foretaste of the joys of heaven above.

125. O LORD OF PERFECT PURITY

Andante religioso. — MEYERBEER.

1. O Lord of per-fect pu-ri-ty, Who dost the world with light a-dorn, And paint the fields of a-zure sky With love-ly hues of eve and morn. True sun up-on our souls a-rise, In beau-ty shin-ing e-vermore; And
2. Up-on our faint-ing souls dis-til The grace of Thy ce-les-tial dew; Let no fresh snare our hearts be-guile, No for-mer sin re-vive a-new. Teach us to knock at heav'n's high door, Teach us the prize of life to win; Teach
3. Be Thou our guide, be Thou our goal, Be Thou our path-way to the skies; Our joy when sor-row fills the soul, In death our e-ver-last-ing prize. Glo-ry to God the Fa-ther be, And to the sole-be-got-ten Son; The

O LORD OF PERFECT PURITY.

The following Hymn may be sung to the same music:

Light of the soul, O Saviour blest,
Soon as Thy presence fills the breast
Darkness and guilt are put to flight,
And all is sweetness and delight.

Son of the Father, Lord most high,
How glad is he who feels Thee nigh!
How sweet in heav'n Thy beam doth glow,
Denied to eye of flesh below!

O Light of light celestial,
O Charity ineffable;
Come in Thy hidden majesty;
Fill us with love, fill us with Thee.

To Jesus from the proud conceal'd,
But evermore to babes reveal'd,
All glory with the Father be,
And Holy Ghost eternally.

THE STAR THAT HERALDS IN THE MORN.

E. Silas

THE STAR THAT HERALDS IN THE MORN.

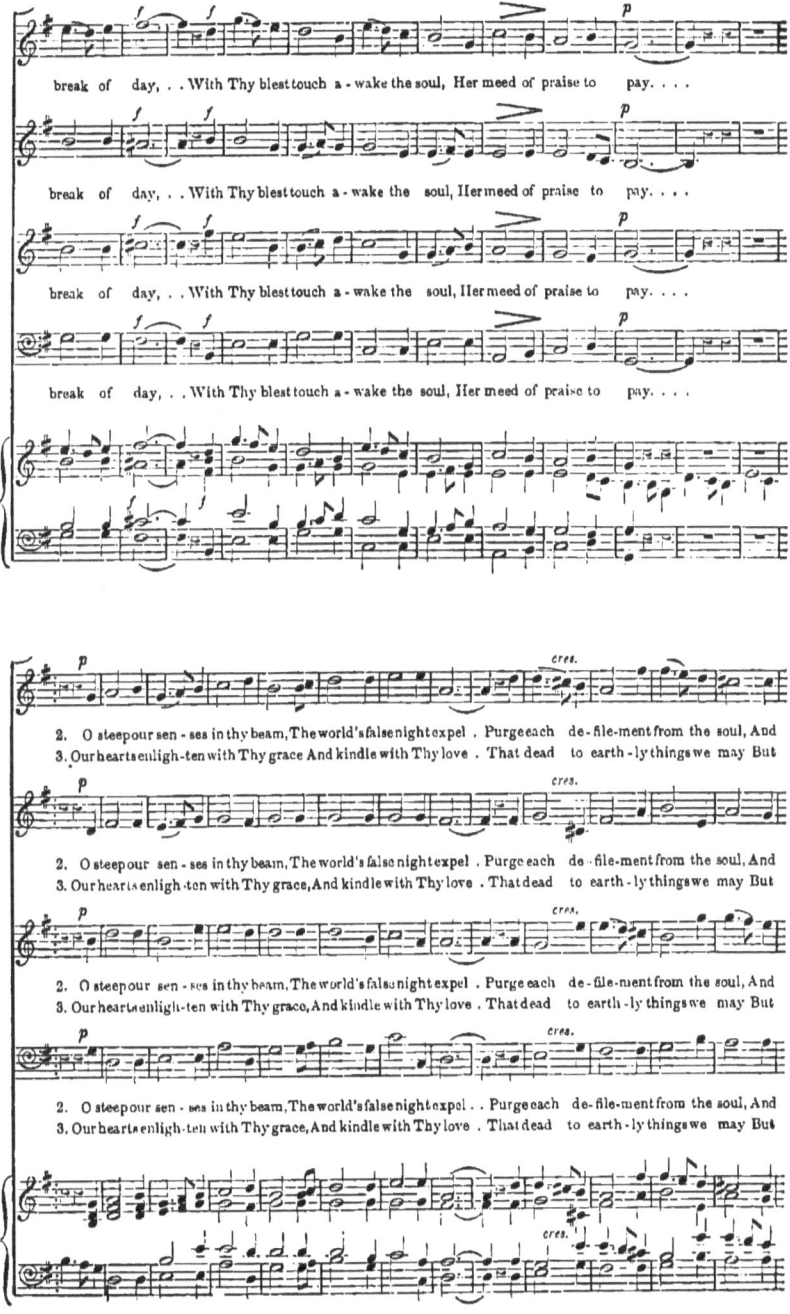

127. NOW DOTH THE SUN ASCEND THE SKY.

AGAIN THE HOLY MORN.

AGAIN THE HOLY MORN.

His new created world
  The Mighty Maker view'd,
With thousand lovely tints adorn'd,
  And straight pronounced it good:
But O, much more He joy'd
  That self-same world to see,
Wash'd in the Lamb's all-saving blood,
  From its impurity.

Nature each day renews,
  Her beauty evermore,
Whence to God's hidden majesty,
  The soul is taught to soar:
But Christ the light of all,
  The Father's image blest,
Gives us to see our God Himself,
  In flesh made manifest.

THE DARKNESS FLEETS.

THE DARKNESS FLEETS.

things to joy a-wake; Oh, may we to thy paths res-tor'd In nature's joy par-take.   A - men.
earth's vast fab-ric bend, While ev-er-more from hearts renew'd New hymns of praise as-cend.   A - men.

The following Hymn may be sung to the same music:

O Brightness of eternal light,
   I worship at Thy feet;
Though all unworthy in Thy sight,
   Thy mercies I repeat.
To save our souls from sin and strife
   Is still Thy work divine;
The gates of everlasting life,
   O gracious Lord, are Thine.

I love to praise Thee when the sun
   Pours forth his early light,
And when the bright stars one by one
   Come twinkling out at night.
If I am free from care and loss,
   I love to praise Thy name;
If I am call'd to bear Thy cross,
   I bless Thee all the same.

If roses on my path I meet,
   I feel the gift is Thine;
If thorns spring up to pierce my feet,
   I still will not repine.
The blessings sent to win my love,
   O Lord, I freely take;
The trials sent my faith to prove,
   I bear for Thy dear sake.

Then let me on my journey go,
   And fear not for the end;
It matters not who is my foe,
   If Jesus be my friend.
In Thee, sweet Lord, I put my trust;
   O guard me while I live;
And when this dust returns to dust,
   My soul in heaven receive.

130. BY THE FIRST BRIGHT EASTER DAY.

1. By the first bright Easter day, When the stone was roll'd away, By the glory round Thee shed, At Thy rising from the dead; King of glory, hear our cry; Make us soon Thy joys to see, Where enthron'd in Majesty, Countless angels sing to Thee.

2.
By Thy parting blessing giv'n
As thou didst ascend to heav'n;
By the cloud of living light
That received Thee out of sight;
  King of glory, &c.

3.
By that rushing sound of might
Coming down from heaven's height
By the cloven tongue of fire,
Holy Ghost, our hearts inspire.
  King of glory, &c.

4.
See the Virgin Mother rise,
Angels bear her to the skies;
Mount aloft, imperial Queen,
Plead on high the cause of men.
  King of glory, &c.

5.
Mary reigns upon the throne
Pre-ordain'd for her alone;
Saints and angels round her sing,
Mother of our God and King.
  King of glory &c.

No. 131, *Accompaniment*, see No. 136.

132. SWEET SAVIOUR! BLESS US ERE WE GO.

For the same in a lower key, see No. 206.

Grant us, dear Lord! from evil ways
True absolution and release ;
And bless us more than in past days
With purity and inward peace.
  Through life's long day, &c.

For all we love,—the poor, the sad,
The sinful,—unto Thee we call !
Oh, let Thy mercy make us glad ;
Thou art our Jesus and our All !
  Through life's long day, &c.

133. SWEET SAVIOUR! BLESS US ERE WE GO.

G. H.
(From a private Collection.)

Sweet Saviour! bless us ere we go; Thy word in-
The day is done, its hours have run; And Thou hast
-to our minds in-stil; And make our luke-warm hearts to glow With
tak-en count of all,— The scan-ty tri-umphs grace hath won, The
low-ly love and fer---vent will.
bro-ken vow, the fre---quent fall.
Through life's long day and
death's dark night, O, gen-tle Je---sus! be... our light!

Grant us, dear Lord! from evil ways
True absolution and release;
And bless us more than in past days
With purity and inward peace.
    Through life's long day, &c.

Do more than pardon,—give us joy,
Sweet fear and sober liberty;
And simple hearts without alloy,
That only long to be like Thee.
    Through life's long day, &c.

Labour is sweet, for Thou hast toiled;
And care is light, for Thou hast cared;
Ah! never let our works be soiled
With strife, or by deceit ensnared.
    Through life's long day, &c.

For all we love, the poor, the sad,
The sinful,—unto Thee, we call;
Oh, let Thy mercy make us glad;
Thou art our Jesus and our All!
    Through life's long day, &c.

134. AS FADES THE GLOWING ORB OF DAY.

135. THE SHADOWS OF THE EVENING HOURS.
(*Evening Hymn.*)

THE SHADOWS OF THE EVENING HOURS.

THE SHADOWS OF THE EVENING HOURS.

1.

The shadows of the evening hours
  Fall from the dark'ning sky;
Upon the fragrance of the flowers
  The dews of evening lie:
Before Thy throne, O Lord of heaven,
  We kneel at close of day;
Look on Thy children from on high,
  And hear us while we pray.

2.

The sorrows of Thy servants, Lord,
  O do not Thou despise;
But let the incense of our prayers
  Before Thy mercy rise.
The brightness of the coming night
  Upon the darkness rolls;
With hopes of future glory chase
  The shadows on our souls.

3.

Let peace, O Lord, Thy peace, O God,
  Upon our souls descend;
From midnight fears and perils Thou
  Our trembling hearts defend.
Give us a respite from our toil;
  Calm and subdue our woes;
Through the long day we suffer, Lord;
  O give us now repose.

136. NOW WITH THE FAST DEPARTING LIGHT.

THE WEST'RING SUN ROLLS DOWN.

THE SUN IS SINKING FAST.

THE SUN IS SINKING FAST.

O JESU, MY BELOVED KING.

141. JESUS, THE VERY THOUGHT OF THEE.
J. RICHARDSON.

JESUS, THE VERY THOUGHT OF THEE.

142. O WHAT IS THIS SPLENDOUR.

J. RICHARDSON.

1. O what is this splen-dour that beams on me now, This beau-ti-ful sun-rise that dawns on my soul? While faint and far-off land and sea lie be-low, And un-der my feet the huge gol-den clouds roll. To what migh-ty King doth this ci-ty be-long, With its rich jew-ell'd shrines and its gar-dens of flow'rs; With its breaths of sweet in-cense, its mea-sures of song, And the light that is gild-ing its num-ber-less tow'rs?

2. See! forth from its gates, like a bri-dal ar-ray, Come the prin-ces of heav'n, how glo-rious they shine! 'Tis to wel-come the stran-ger, to show me the way, And tell me that all I see round me is mine. But words may not tell of the vi-sion of peace, With its wor-ship-ful seem-ing, its mar-vel-lous fires; Where the soul is at large, where its sor-rows all cease, And the gift has out-bid-den its bold-est de-sires!

No. **143**, *Accompaniment*, see No. 72.

No. **144**, *Accompaniment*, see No. 130.

145. IN HEAVEN 'TIS GIVEN TO REST THEE.

J. R. Schachner

No. **146**, *Accompaniment*, see No. 129.

I DWELL A CAPTIVE IN THIS HEART.

No. 148, Accompaniment, see No. 104.

Yes, Heaven is the Prize!
When sorrows press around,
Look up beyond the skies
Where hope and strength are found.
    'Tis Heaven, &c.

Yes, Heaven is the Prize!
Oh, 'tis not hard to gain,
He surely wins who tries ;—
For hope can conquer pain.
    'Tis Heaven, &c.

Yes, Heaven is the Prize!
The strife will soon be past,
Faint not! but raise your eyes
And struggle to the last.
    'Tis Heaven, &c.

Yes, Heaven is the Prize!
Faith shows the crown to gain,—
Hope lights the way, and dies—
But Love will always reign.
    'Tis Heaven, &c.

Yes, Heaven is the Prize!
Too much cannot be given,
And he alone is wise
Who gives up *all* for Heaven.
    'Tis Heaven, &c.

Yes, Heaven is the Prize!
Death opens wide the door,
And then the Spirit flies
To God for evermore.
    'Tis Heaven, &c.

152. O GOD OF ORPHANS! HEAR OUR PRAYER.

Sleep, holy Babe,
Oh, snatch thy brief repose;
Too quickly will thy slumber break,
And thou to lengthen'd pains awake,
Which death alone shall close.

Then must those hands
Which now so small I see,
Those feet so lovely and divine,
That flesh so delicately fine,
Be pierced and rent for me!

Then must that brow
Its thorny crown receive;
That cheek, more lovely than the rose,
Be drench'd with blood, and marr'd with blows
That I thereby may live!

O Lady blest!
To thee I suppliant cry;
Forgive the wrong that I have done
In causing by my sins thy Son
Upon the Cross to die.

O Jesu Lord!
By thy sweet childhood's years,
Blot out from their terrific page
My sins of youth and later age,
In these my contrite tears.

So may I sing
Immortal praise to thee,
Who, once a Babe of human birth,
Now reignest Lord of heaven and earth,
Through all eternity.

154. SEE! AMID THE WINTER'S SNOW.
(CHRISTMAS CAROL.)

Adapted from DOWLAND.

See! a-mid the win-ter's snow, Born for us on earth be-low; See! the ten-der Lamb ap-pears, Pro-mis'd from e-ter-nal years.
Lo! with-in a man-ger lies He who built the earth and skies: He who thron'd in height sub-lime, Sits a-mid the che-ru-bim.
Say, ye ho-ly shep-herds, say, What your joy-ful news to-day? Where-fore have you left your sheep On the lone-ly moun-tain steep?
As we watch'd at dead of night, Lo! we saw a won-drous light; An-gels sing-ing, Peace on earth, Told us of the Sa-viour's birth.

Chorus.
Hail, thou e-ver bless-ed morn! Hail, Re-demp-tion's hap-py dawn! Sing through all Je-ru-sa-lem, Christ is born in Beth-le-hem!

Sacred Infant, all divine,
What a tender love was Thine,
Thus to come from highest bliss,
Down to such a world as this!
      Hail, &c.

Virgin Mother! Mary blest!
By the joys that fill thy breast,
Pray for us, that we may prove
Worthy of the Saviour's love.
      Hail, &c.

Teach, oh, teach us, holy Child,
By Thy face so meek and mild
Teach us to resemble Thee
In Thy sweet humility!
      Hail, &c.

* Omit Chorus here, and, if possible, let the next verse be sung by a few select voices.

LEAD ME TO THY PEACEFUL MANGER.

157. O COME AND MOURN WITH ME A WHILE.

J. RICHARDSON.

O come and mourn with me a while; See, Mary calls us to her side; Oh, come and let us mourn with her: Jesus, our Love, is crucified!

Have we no tears to shed for Him, While soldiers scoff and Jews deride? Ah, look how patiently He hangs: Jesus, our Love, is crucified!

A - men.

Seven times He spoke, seven words of love,
And all three hours His silence cried
For mercy on the souls of men:
Jesus, our Love, is crucified!

Come, take thy stand beneath the Cross,
And let the Blood from out that Side
Fall gently on thee drop by drop:
Jesus, our Love, is crucified!

A broken heart, a fount of tears,
Ask, and they will not be denied;
A broken heart love's cradle is:
Jesus, our Love, is crucified!

O Love of God! O Sin of Man!
In this dread act your strength is tried;
And victory remains with love,
For He, our Love, is crucified!

158. AT THE CROSS HER STATION KEEPING.

(STABAT MATER.)

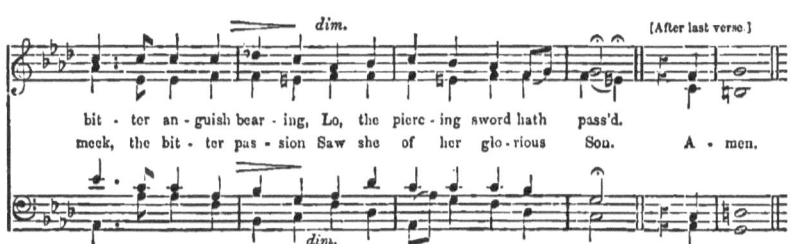

Who could mark, from tears refraining,
Christ's dear Mother uncomplaining,
 In so great a sorrow bow'd?
Who unmov'd behold her languish,
Underneath His Cross of anguish,
 'Mid the fierce unpitying crowd?

In His people's sins rejected,
She her Jesus, unprotected,
 Saw with thorns, with scourges rent:
Saw her Son from judgment taken,
Her belov'd in death forsaken,
 Till His spirit forth He sent.

159. MY JESUS! SAY WHAT WRETCH HAS DARED?

G. H.
(*From a private Collection.*)

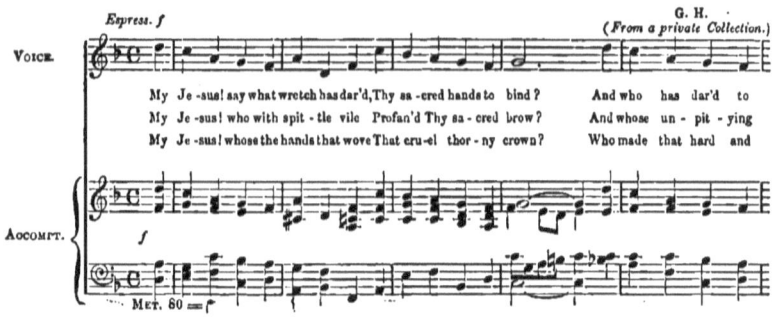

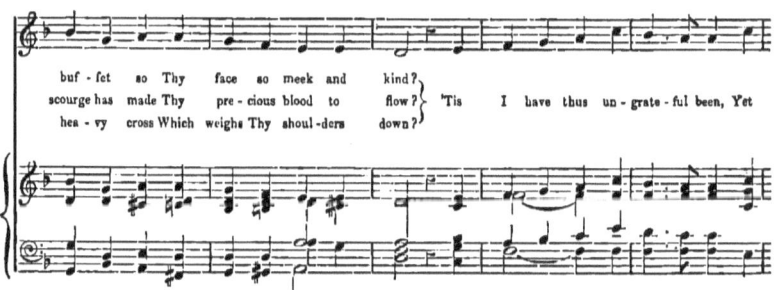

My Jesus! who has mocked Thy thirst
   With vinegar and gall;
Who held the nails that pierced Thy hands,
   And made the hammer fall? ('Tis I, &c.)

My Jesus! say, who dared to nail
   Those tender feet of Thine;
And whose the arm that raised the lance
   To pierce that Heart divine? ('Tis I, &c.)

And, Mary! who has murdered thus,
   Thy loved and only One?
Canst thou forgive the blood-stained hand
   That robbed thee of thy Son?

'Tis I have thus ungrateful been,
   To Jesus and to thee;
Forgive me for thy Jesus' sake,
   And pray to Him for me.

160. HAIL! CROSS MOST SWEET AND HOLY.

BACH.

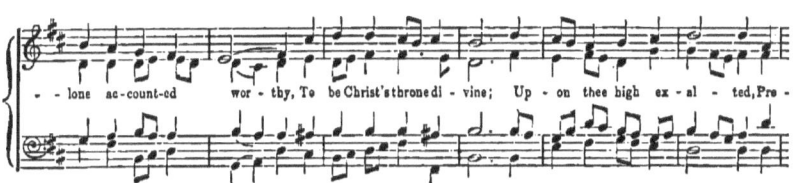

Hail! Stair of sinners' pathway
Which led heav'n's King on high,
That to the choir of angels
Man also might draw nigh;
Here did the Son of David,
Life's author, life restore,
And bear this shame, that mortals
Might live for evermore.

Hail! Seal of God's new covenant,
And banner of the King,
Where, for the sheep the shepherd,
Himself made offering;
And He shall be our leader
Unto the realms of day,
Whose precious Blood hath hallow'd
His blessed Cross for aye.

161. HAIL JESUS! HAIL! WHO FOR MY SAKE.

To endless ages let us praise
The Precious Blood, whose price could raise
  The world from wrath and sin ;
Whose streams our inward thirst appease,
And heal the sinner's worst disease,
  If he but bathe therein.

O sweetest Blood, that can implore
Pardon of God, and heaven restore,
  The heaven which sin had lost :
While Abel's blood for vengeance pleads,
What Jesus shed still intercedes
  For those who wrong Him most.

Oh, to be sprinkled from the wells
Of Christ's own Sacred Blood, excels
  Earth's best and highest bliss :
The ministers of wrath divine
Hurt not the happy hearts that shine
  With those red drops of His !

Ah ! there is joy amid the Saints,
And hell's despairing courage faints
  When this sweet song we raise :
O louder then, and louder still,
Earth with one mighty chorus fill,
  The Precious Blood to praise !

Blest through endless ages,
  Be the precious stream ;
Which from endless torment,
  Did the world redeem ;
There the fainting spirit,
  Drinks of life her fill ;
There as in a fountain,
  Laves herself at will.

Oft as earth exulting,
  Wafts its praise on high ;
Hell with terror trembles,
  Heav'n is fill'd with joy.
Lift ye then, your voices,
  Swell the mighty flood ;
Louder still, and louder,
  Praise the Precious Blood.

163. WHY IS THY FACE SO LIT WITH SMILES.
(THE ASCENSION.)

J. F. BARNETT

Why is thy face so lit with smiles, O bles-sed Mo-ther! Why? And
Mo-ther! how canst thou smile to-day? How can thine eyes be bright, When

where-fore is thy beam-ing look So fix'd up-on the sky? From
He, thy Life, thy Love, thine All, Hath va-nish'd from thy sight? The

out thine o-ver-flow-ing eyes Bright lights of glad-ness part, As
Feet which thou hast kiss'd so oft, Those liv-ing Feet, are gone; And

though some gush-ing fount of joy Had bro-ken in thy heart.
now thou canst but stoop and kiss Their print up-on the stone.

Yes! He hath left thee, Mother dear!
His throne is far above;
How canst thou be so full of joy,
When thou hast lost thy love?
Ah no! thy love is rightful love,
From all selfseeking free;
The change that is such gain to Him
Can be no loss to thee!

'Tis sweet to feel our Saviour's love,
To feel His Presence near;
Yet loyal love His glory holds
A thousand times more dear.
Ah! never is our love so pure,
As when refined by pain,
Or when God's glory upon earth
Finds in our loss its gain.

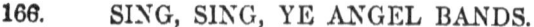

166. SING, SING, YE ANGEL BANDS.

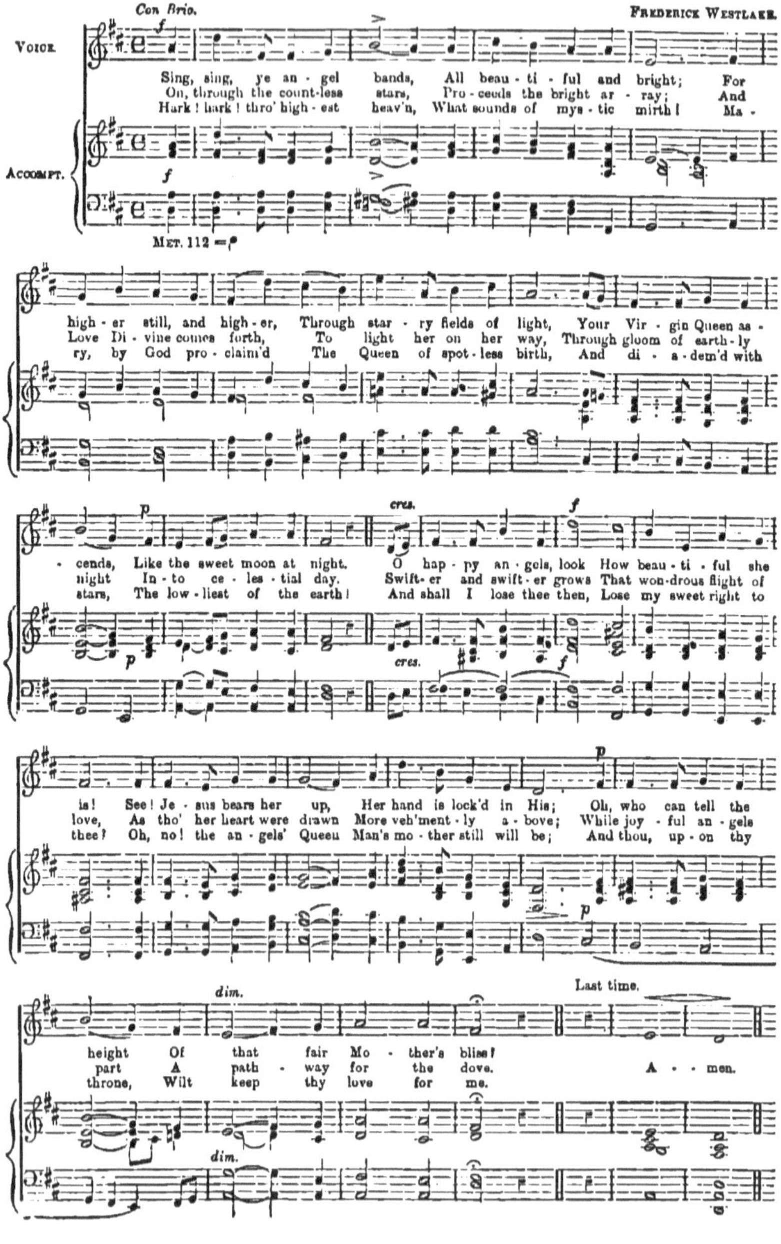
Con Brio.
FREDERICK WESTLAKE.
Voice
Accompt.
Met. 112 =
Sing, sing, ye an - gel bands, All beau - ti - ful and bright; For
On, through the count-less stars, Pro - ceeds the bright ar - ray; And
Hark! hark! thro' high - est heav'n, What sounds of mys - tic mirth! Ma -
high - er still, and high - er, Through star - ry fields of light, Your Vir - gin Queen as -
Love Di - vine comes forth, To light her on her way, Through gloom of earth - ly
ry, by God pro - claim'd The Queen of spot - less birth, And di - a - dem'd with
- cends, Like the sweet moon at night. O hap - py an - gels, look How beau - ti - ful she
night In - to ce - les - tial day. Swift - er and swift - er grows That won-drous flight of
stars, The low - liest of the earth! And shall I lose thee then, Lose my sweet right to
is! See! Je - sus bears her up, Her hand is lock'd in His; Oh, who can tell the
love, As tho' her heart were drawn More veh'ment - ly a - bove; While joy - ful an - gels
thee? Oh, no! the an - gels' Queen Man's mo - ther still will be; And thou, up - on thy
height Of that fair Mo - ther's bliss!
part A path - way for the dove.
throne, Wilt keep thy love for me.
Last time.
A - - men.
cres.
dim.

UPLIFT THE VOICE AND SING.

Ma-ry, end-less praise! Raise your joy-ful voi-ces, raise! Praise to God who reigns a-bove, Who has made her for His love.

To be with God on high,
 Her heart was all on fire;
She sought and ask'd to die,
 With humble, sweet desire.
  Praise to Mary, &c.

At length her Heavenly Spouse,
 Who loved her with such love,
Invites her to repose
 With Him in heaven above.
  Praise to Mary, &c.

Then came sweet Love from heaven,
 And, with his flaming dart,
The mortal wound was given
 To Mary's stainless heart.
  Praise to Mary, &c.

Then did that beauteous Dove
 Spring joyfully on high;
Her Son receives with love,
 And bears her to the sky.
  Praise to Mary, &c.

And now, bright Queen of Love!
 While seated on thy throne,
High in the realms above,
 Near to thy glorious Son,
  Praise to Mary, &c.

Hear, from that blest abode,
 A sinner cries to thee:
Teach me to love that God
 Who bears such love to me.
  Praise to Mary, &c.

168. HAIL, BRIGHT STAR OF OCEAN!

J. RICHARDSON.

HAIL, BRIGHT STAR OF OCEAN!

Break the captive's fetters;
   Light on blindness pour;
All our ills expelling,
   Ev'ry bliss implore.

Shew thyself a mother;
   May the Word divine,
Born for us thine Infant,
   Hear our prayers through thine!

Virgin all excelling,
   Mildest of the mild,
Freed from guilt, preserve us
   Meek and undefiled.

Keep our life all spotless,
   Make our way secure,
Till we find in Jesus
   Joy for evermore.

† Through the highest heaven,
   To the Almighty Three,
Father, Son, and Spirit,
   One same glory be.

† This stanza may be sung to the first part of the music to ✳, ending with "**Amen.**"

HAIL! BRIGHT STAR OF OCEAN.

HAIL! BRIGHT STAR OF OCEAN.

171. STAR OF JACOB, EVER BEAMING!

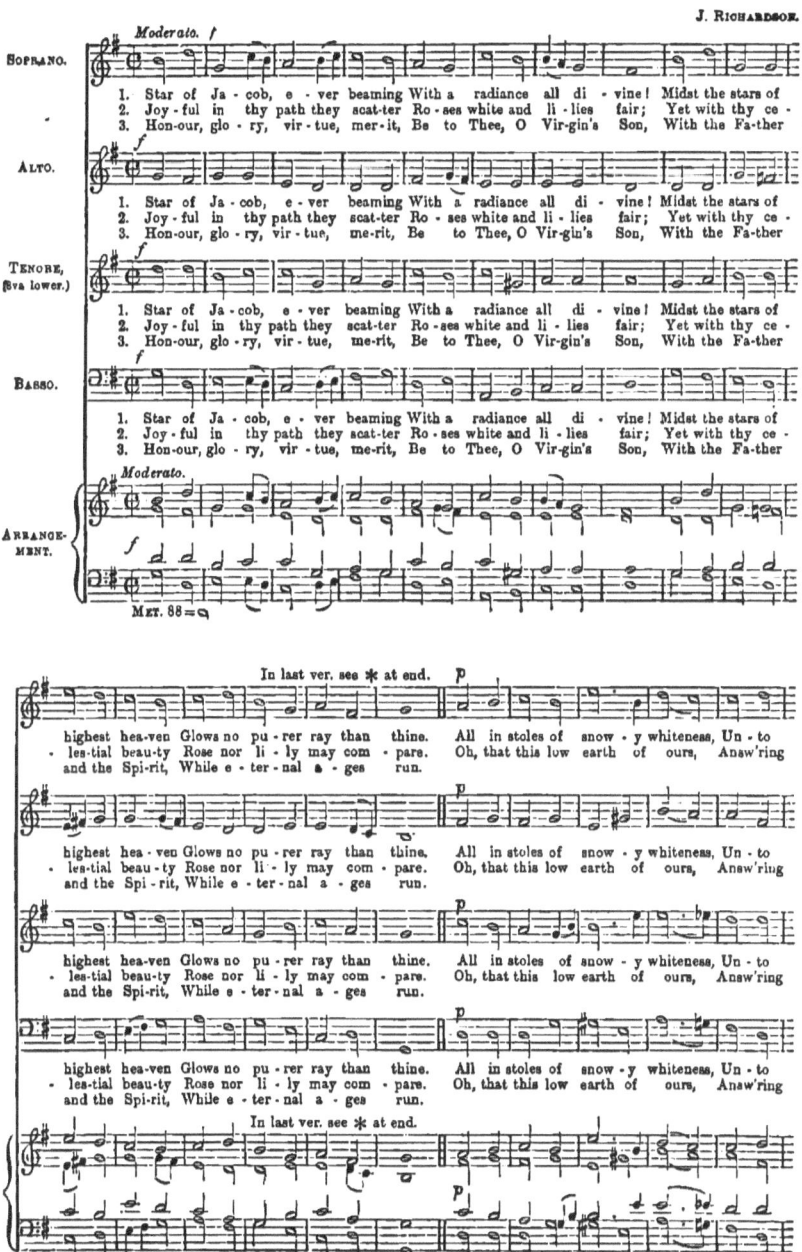

STAR OF JACOB, EVER BEAMING

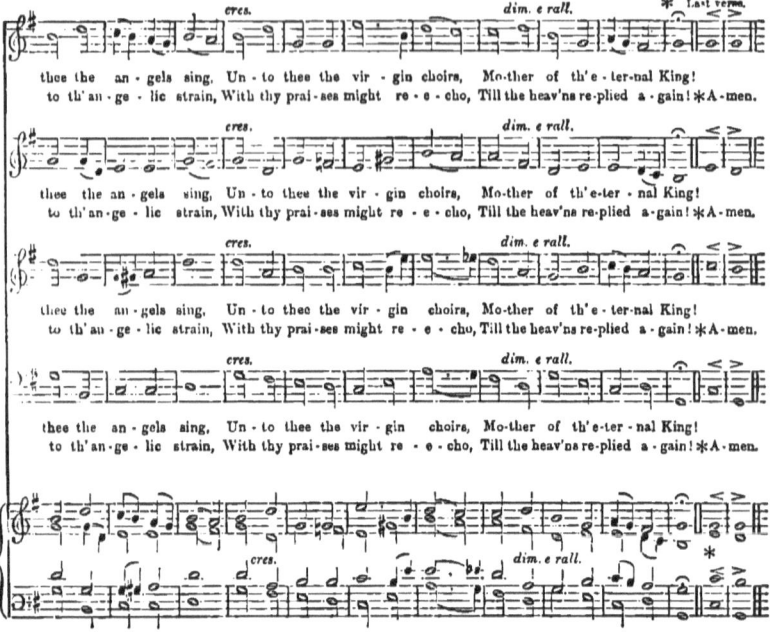

The following Hymn may be sung to the same music:—

SPOTLESS ANNA! Juda's glory!
    Through the Church from east to west,
Ev'ry tongue proclaims thy praises,
    Holy Mary's Mother blest!

Saintly Kings and priestly Sires
    Blended in thy sacred line;
Thou in virtue, all before thee
    Didst excel by grace divine.

Link'd in bonds of purest wedlock,
    Thine it was for us to bear.
By the favour of High Heaven,
    Our eternal Virgin Star.

From thy stem, in beauty budded
    Ancient Jesse's mystic rod;
Earth from thee received the Mother
    Of th' Almighty Son of God.

† Honour, glory, virtue, merit,
    Be to thee, O Virgin's Son,
With the Father and the Spirit,
    While eternal ages run.

† This stanza may be sung to the first part of the music to ✶, ending with "Amen."

172. MOTHER OF MERCY.

Ah, little know they of thy worth
Who would deny thy love to me;
For what did Jesus love on earth
One-half so tenderly as thee?

Oh, gain me grace to love thee more;
Thy Son will give if thou wilt plead:
And, Mother, when life's cares are o'er,
Oh, I shall love thee then indeed.

My Lord, when His three hours were run,
Bequeath'd thee from the cross to me;
And oh, how can I love thy Son,
Sweet Mother, if I love not thee?

173. HAIL, QUEEN OF HEAVEN!

FREDERICK WESTLAKE

Sojourners in this vale of tears,
To thee, blest Advocate, we cry;
Pity our sorrows, calm our fears,
And soothe with hope our misery.
Refuge in grief, Star of the sea,
Pray for the mourner, pray for me.

And while to Him who reigns above,
In Godhead One, in Persons Three,
The source of life, of grace, of love,
Homage we pay on bended knee;
Do thou, bright Queen, Star of the sea,
Pray for thy children, pray for me.

174. OH! BALMY AND BRIGHT.
(A MAY CAROL.)

WILHELM SCHULTHES.

OH! BALMY AND BRIGHT.

175. THE MOON IS IN THE HEAVENS ABOVE.

Oh thou art bright as bright can be,
As bountiful as thou art bright ;
And welcome is the thought of thee,
As fragrance of an eastern night.
　　Our hands, &c.

Calm as the blessed eye of God,
When looking o'er this world below,
He bids thee shed His peace abroad,
A secret balm for every woe.
　　Our hands, &c.

By thee we gain, dear spotless Queen !
Some glimpse of what our God must be ;
And in thy glory His is seen,
He shows Himself when He shows thee !
　　Our hands, &c.

176. O VISION BRIGHT!

O vision bright!
Th' eternal light
Of the dear Son may we descry;
Where, brighter far
Than moon or star,
Mary, our Mother, reigns on high.

O vision bright!
In softest flight
The Dove around His Spouse doth fly;
Where, in that height
Of matchless light,
Mary, our Mother, reigns on high.

O vision bright!
Angel's delight!
The Mother sits with Jesus nigh:
Her form He bears,
Her look he wears;
Mary, our Mother, reigns on high.

O vision bright!
Life's darkest night
Is fair as dawn when thou art nigh;
Where, 'mid the throng
Of psalm and song,
Mary, our Mother, reigns on high.

177. LOOK DOWN, O MOTHER MARY!

J. RICHARDSON.

LOOK DOWN, O MOTHER MARY!

O Mary, dearest Mother!
 If thou wouldst have us live,
Say that we are thy children,
 And Jesus will forgive.

Our sins make us unworthy
 That title still to bear,
But thou art still our Mother;—
 Then shew a Mother's care.

Unfold to us thy mantle;
 There stay we without fear:
What evil can befall us
 If, Mother, thou art near?

O kindest, dearest Mother!
 Thy sinful children save;
Look down on us with pity,
 Who thy protection crave.

Repeat ver. 1, "Look down," &c., to "love," ending with "Amen."

The following Hymn may be sung to the same music:—

Hail, thou resplendent star
 That shinest o'er the main;
Blest Mother of our God,
 And ever-virgin Queen!

Hail, happy gate of bliss,
 Greeted by Gabriel's tongue!
Obtain for us true peace,
 And cancel Eva's wrong.

Loosen the sinner's bands,
 All evils drive away;
Bring light unto the blind,
 And for all graces pray.

Exert the Mother's care,
 And us thy children own;
To Him convey our prayer
 Who chose to be thy Son.

O pure, O spotless Maid!
 Whose meekness all surpass'd,
Our lusts and passions quell,
 And make us mild and chaste.

Preserve our lives unstain'd,
 And guide us in the way;
Until we come to thee,
 To joys that ne'er decay.

† Praise to the Father be,
 With Christ, His only Son,
And to the Holy Ghost,
 Thrice blessed Three in One.

† This verse to first part of music, down to ✱, ending with "Amen."

178. LOOK DOWN, O MOTHER MARY.

1 Look down, O Mother Mary, From Thy bright throne above, Cast down upon Thy children, One only glance of love, And if a heart so tender, With pity flow not o'er, Then turn away, O Mother, And look on us no more.

2 See how, ungrateful sinners,
　We stand before thy Son;
His loving Heart upbraids us
　The evil we have done.
But if thou wilt appease Him,
　Speak for us but one word;
Thou only canst obtain us
　The pardon of our Lord.

3 O Mary, dearest Mother,
　If thou wouldst have us live
Say that we are thy children,
　And Jesus will forgive.
Our sins make us unworthy
　That title still to bear,
But thou art still our Mother;
　Then show a Mother's care.

4 Unfold to us thy mantle;
　There stay we without fear
What evil can befall us
　If, Mother, thou art near?
O kindest, dearest Mother,
　Thy sinful children save;
Look down on us with pity,
　Who thy protection crave.

HEAR THY CHILDREN, GENTLEST MOTHER.

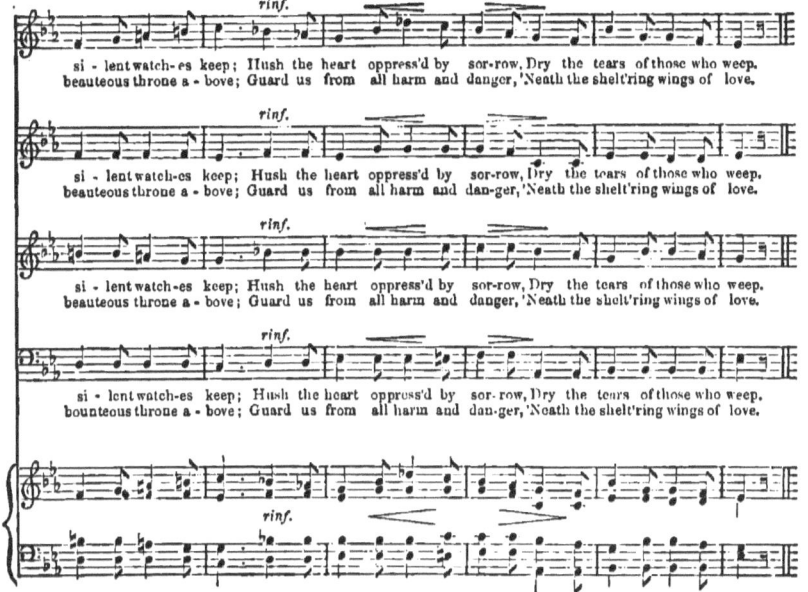

The following Hymn may be sung to the same music:

Hear Thy children, gentle Jesus,
  While we breathe our evening prayer;
Save us from all harm and danger,
  Take us 'neath Thy shelt'ring care.

Save us from the wiles of Satan,
  'Mid the lone and sleepful night,
Sweetly may bright guardian angels
  Keep us 'neath their watchful sight.

Gentle Jesus, look in pity
  From Thy great white throne above,
All the night Thy Heart is wakeful
  In Thy sacrament of love.

Shades of even fast are falling,
  Day is fading into gloom;
When the shades of death fall round us,
  Lead Thine exiled children home.

No. 180, *Accompaniment*, see No. 157.

No. 182, *Accompaniment*, see No. 155.

183. HOLY QUEEN, WE BEND BEFORE THEE.

Adapted from GLUCK.

Holy Queen, we bend before thee, Queen of purity divine; Make us love thee, we implore thee, Make us truly to be thine. Unto thee a Child was given, Greater than the sons of men; Coming down from highest heaven, To create the world again. Amen.

Thou by faith the gates unfolding Of the kingdom in the skies, Hast to us, by faith beholding, Shewn the land of Paradise. Thou, when deepest night infernal Had for ages shrouded man, Gav'st us that light eternal Promis'd when the world began.

Teach, oh, teach us, holy Mother,
　How to conquer ev'ry sin,
How to love and help each other,
　How the prize of life to win:
Teach us how all earthly pleasures,
　All the world's enchanting bloom,
Are outrivall'd by the treasures
　Of the glorious world to come.

Oh, by that Almighty Maker,
　Whom thyself, a virgin, bore;
Oh, by thy supreme Creator,
　Link'd with thee for evermore,—
By the hope thy name inspires,
　By our doom reversed through thee,
Bring us, Queen of angel quires
　To a blest eternity!

184. RAISE YOUR VOICES, VALES AND MOUNTAINS.

Frederick Westlake.

RAISE YOUR VOICES, VALES AND MOUNTAINS.

No. 185, *Accompaniment*, see No. 162.

THE JOYFUL MYSTERIES.

J. RICHARDSON.

By th' Arch-an-gel's word of love That announc'd Thee from a-bove; By the grace to Ma-ry giv'n; By Thy first de-scent from heav'n; Child of Ma-ry, hear our cry; Thou wert help-less once as we; Now en-thron'd in ma-jes-ty, .. Count-less an-gels sing to Thee.

By that journey made in haste
O'er the desert mountain waste;
By that voice whose heav'nly tone
Thrill'd the Baptist in the womb;
   Child of Mary, &c.

By Thy poor and lowly lot,
By the manger and the grot,
By Thy tender feet and hands
Folded in their swaddling bands
   Child of Mary, &c.

By the joy of Simeon blest
When he clasp'd Thee to his breast;
By the widow'd Anna's song
Pour'd amid the wondering throng;
   Child of Mary, &c.

By our Lady's glad delight,
In her temple, at the sight
Of her Child so young and fair,
Wiser than the wisest there;
   Child of Mary, &c.

187. THE JOYFUL MYSTERIES.

4
By the joy of Simeon blest,
When he clasp'd Thee to his breast;
By the widow'd Anna's song,
Pour'd amid the wondering throng.
    Child of Mary, &c.

5
By our Lady's glad delight,
In the temple, at the sight
Of her child so young and fair,
Wiser than the wisest there.
    Child of Mary, &c.

188. THE SORROWFUL MYSTERIES.

1. By the Blood that flow'd from Thee, In Thy griev-ous a-go-ny,
2. By the cords that round Thee cast, Bound Thee to the pil-lar fast,
3. By the thorns that crown'd Thy head, By Thy scep-tre of a reed,

By the trai-tor's guile-ful kiss, Fil-ling up Thy bit-ter-ness.
By the scourge so meek-ly borne, By Thy pur-ple robe of scorn.
By Thy foes on bend-ing knee, Mock-ing at Thy roy-al-ty.

Je-sus, Sa-viour, hear our cry, Thou wert suf-fring once as we, Now enthron'd in ma-jes-ty, Count-less an-gels sing to Thee. A-men.

4.
By the people's cruel jeers,
By the holy womens' tears,
By Thy footsteps faint and slow,
Weigh'd beneath Thy cross of woe.
  Jesus, Saviour, &c.

5.
By Thy weeping Mother's woe,
By the sound that pierc'd her through,
When in anguish standing by,
On the cross she saw Thee die.
  Jesus, Saviour, &c.

189. THE GLORIOUS MYSTERIES.

(See also 130A.) *Adapted from* MENDELSSOHN.

1. By the first bright Eas-ter-day, When the stone was roll'd a-way, By the glo-ry round Thee shed, At Thy ris-ing from the dead.
2. By thy part-ing bless-ing giv'n, As Thou did'st as-cend to heav'n; By the cloud of liv-ing light, That re-ceiv'd Thee out of sight.
3. By that rush-ing sound of might, Com-ing down from hea-ven's height; By the clo-ven tongue of fire, Ho-ly Ghost our hearts in-spire.

King of glo-ry, hear our cry,.. Make us soon Thy joys to see, Where en-thron'd in ma-jes-ty, Count-less an-gels sing to Thee. A-men.

4
See the Virgin Mother rise,
Angels bear her to the skies;
Mount aloft imperial queen,
Plead on high the cause of men.
   King of glory, &c.

5
Mary reigns upon the throne,
Pre-ordained for her alone;
Saints and angels round her sing,
Mother of our God and King.
   King of glory, &c.

THE JOYOUS BIRDS ARE SINGING.

191. HAIL! HOLY JOSEPH, HAIL!

J. R. Schachner.

HAIL! HOLY JOSEPH, HAIL!

192. # SEEK YE THE GRACE OF GOD.

(ST. JOSEPH.)

MEYER LUTZ.

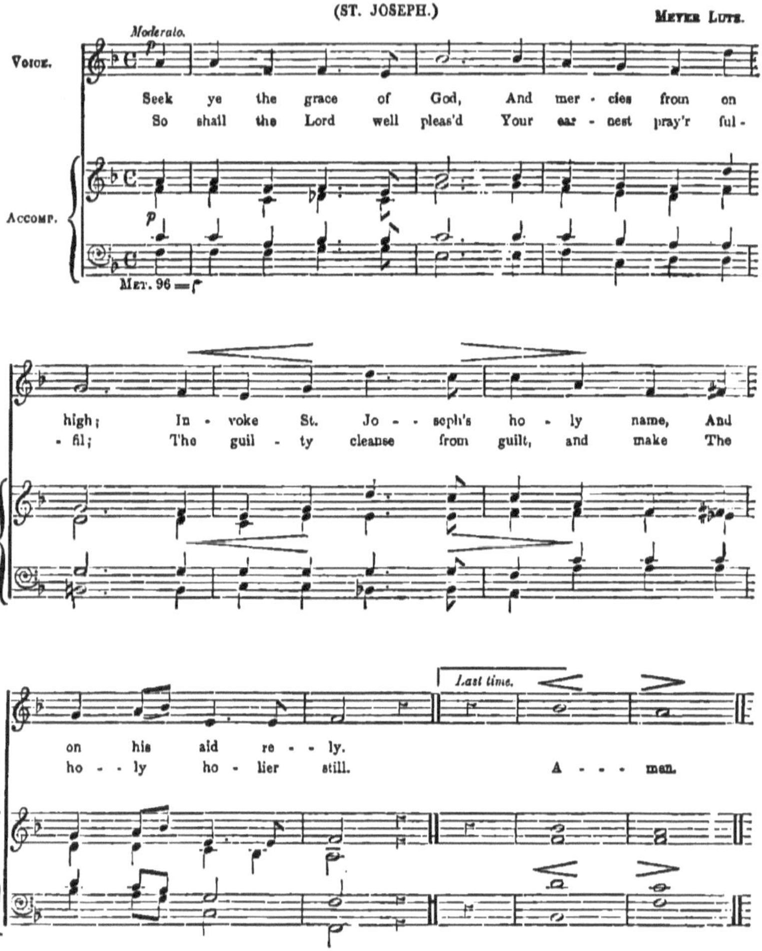

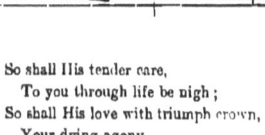

Moderato.
Voice.
Accomp.
Met. 96 =
Seek ye the grace of God, And mer - cies from on high; In - voke St. Jo - - seph's ho - ly name, And on his aid re - - - ly.
So shall the Lord well pleas'd Your ear - nest pray'r ful - - fil; The guil - ty cleanse from guilt, and make The ho - - ly ho - lier still.
Last time.
A - - - men.

So shall His tender care,
To you through life be nigh;
So shall His love with triumph crown,
Your dying agony.

Hail! mightiest of Saints,
To whom submissive bent
He whose Creator-hand outstretched,
The starry firmament

Hail! Mary's spouse elect,
Hail! Guardian of the Word!
Nurse of the Highest, and esteemed,
The Father of the Lord!

Blest Trinity, to Thee,
From all in earth and heaven,
And to St. Joseph's holy name,
Be praise and honour given!

193. LOVELY FLOWERS OF MARTYRS, HAIL!
(HOLY INNOCENTS)

Lovely flow'rs of martyrs hail! Smitten by the tyrant foe On life's threshold,—as the gale Strews the roses ere they blow.

First to die for Christ's sweet lambs, At the very altar ye, With your fatal crowns and palms, Sport in your simplicity.

Honour, virtue, glory, merit, Be to Thee, O Virgin's Son, With the Father and the Spirit, While eternal ages run. Amen.

The following hymn may be sung to the same music:—

Mother of our Lord and Saviour,
    First in beauty as in power!
Glory of the Christian nations,
    Ready help in trouble's hour!

Nought can hurt the pure in spirit,
    Who upon thine aid rely;
At thy hand secure of gaining
    Strength and mercy from on high.

Safe beneath thy mighty shelter,
    Though a thousand hosts combine,
All must fall or flee before us,
    Scattered by His arm divine.

Through the everlasting ages,
    Blessed Trinity, to Thee,
Father, Son, and Holy Spirit,
    Praise and endless glory be.

195. SAINT OF THE SACRED HEART.
(ST. JOHN THE EVANGELIST.)

FREDERICK WESTLAKE.

Saint of the Sa-cred Heart, Sweet teach-er of the Word, Part-ner of
We know not all thy gifts, But Christ this bids us see, That He who
Dear Saint! I stand far off, With sin and shame op-press'd, Oh, may I

Ma-ry's woes, And fa-v'rite of thy Lord! Thou to whom grace was giv'n To
so lov'd all, Found more to love in thee. When the last eve-ning came, Thy
dare, like thee, To lean up-on His breast? The gifts He gave to thee, He

stand when Pe-ter fell; Whose heart could brook the cross Of Him it lov'd so well!
head was on His breast, Pil-low'd on earth, where now In Heav'n the saints find rest.
gave thee to im-part, And I, too, claim with thee His Mo-ther and His Heart!

No. 196, *Accompaniment*, see No. 78.

THE HEATHEN MONARCH SITS ENTHRONED.

198. FAITH OF OUR FATHERS.

Faith of our Fathers! living still, In spite of dungeon, fire, and sword: Oh, how our hearts beat high with joy When e'er we hear that glorious word: Faith of our Fathers! Holy Faith! We will be true to thee till death!

Our Fathers, chain'd in prisons dark, Were still in heart and conscience free; How sweet would be their children's fate, If they, like them, could die for thee! Faith of our Fathers! Holy Faith! We will be true to thee till death!

Faith of our Fathers! Mary's prayers
Shall win our country back to thee;
And through the truth that comes from God,
Oh, then indeed we shall be free.
Faith of our Fathers! Holy Faith!
We will be true to thee till death!

Faith of our Fathers! we will love
Both friend and foe in all our strife:
And preach thee too, as love knows how,
By kindly words and virtuous life.
Faith of our Fathers! Holy Faith!
We will be true to thee till death!

199. O BLESSED FATHER! SENT BY GOD.

(ST. VINCENT DE PAUL.)

J. RICHARDSON.

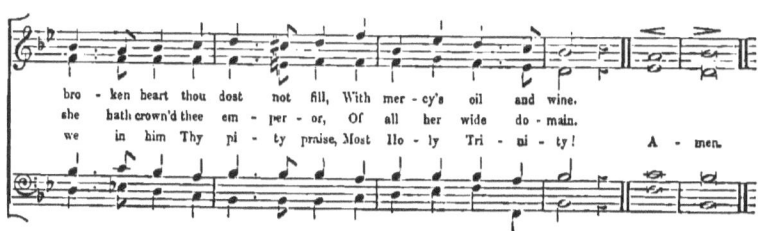

200. THOU CROWN OF ALL THE VIRGIN CHOIR!
(FEASTS OF VIRGINS.)

201. O LORD OF LIGHT, ONE GLANCE OF THINE.

(ST. MARY MAGDALENE.)

MEYER LUTZ.

No. 202, *Accompaniment*, see No. 155.

204. HAIL, GABRIEL! HAIL!

(ST. GABRIEL.)

J. RICHARDSON.

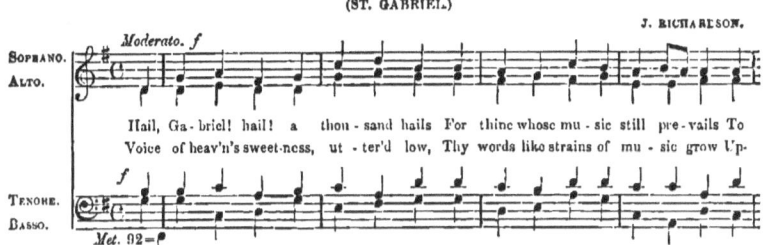

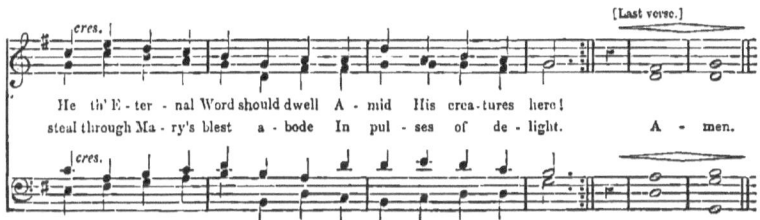

O Voice! dear Voice! the ages hear
That Hail of thine still ling'ring near,
 An unexhausted song;
And still thou com'st with balmy wing,
And, oh! thou seemest still to sing,
 Thine Ave to prolong.

Take up in Heaven for us thy part,
And, singing to the Sacred Heart,
 Thy strains of rapture raise;
And tune with endless Ave still
The voices of the blest, and fill
 The ear of God with praise!

205. MICHAEL, PRINCE OF HIGHEST HEAVEN.

(HOLY ANGELS.)

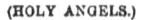

METER LUTZ.

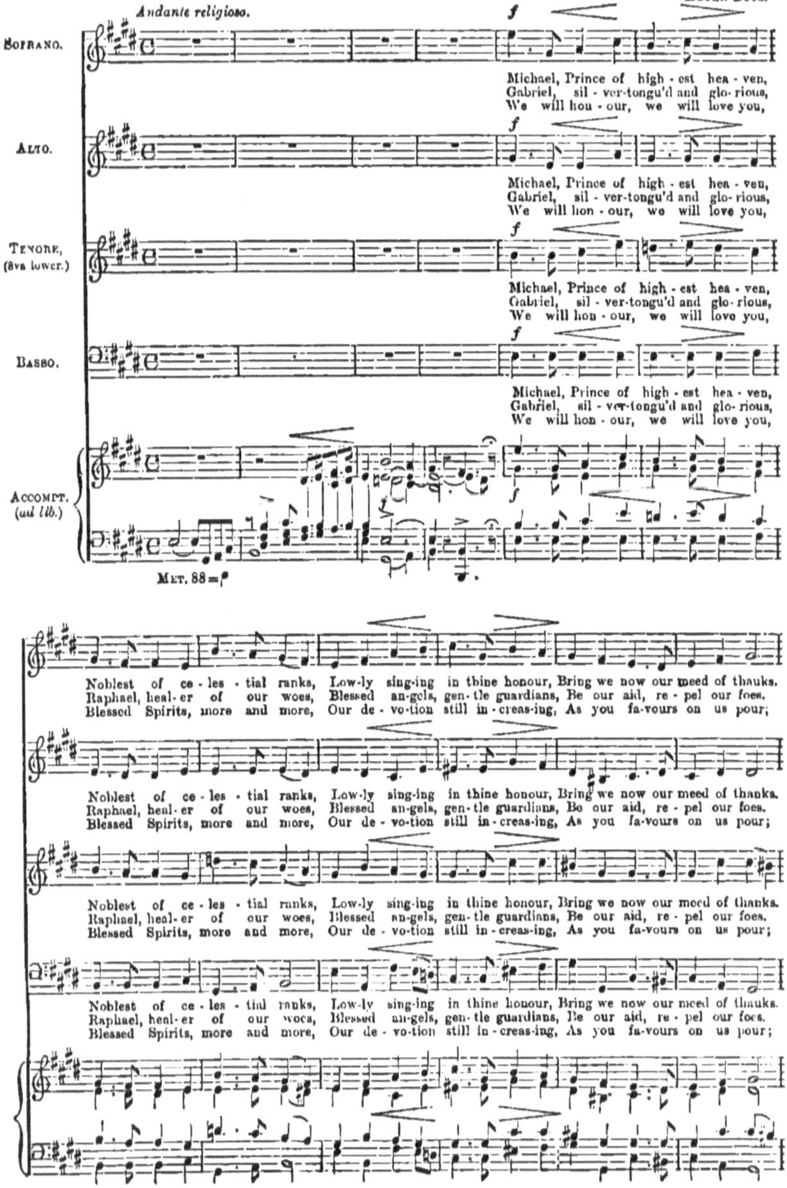
Andante religioso.
SOPRANO.
ALTO.
TENORE, (8va lower.)
BASSO.
ACCOMPT. (ad lib.)
MET. 88 =
Michael, Prince of high - est hea - ven,
Gabriel, sil - ver-tongu'd and glo - rious,
We will hon - our, we will love you,
Noblest of ce - les - tial ranks, Low-ly sing-ing in thine honour, Bring we now our meed of thanks.
Raphael, heal- er of our woes, Blessed an-gels, gen- tle guardians, Be our aid, re - pel our foes.
Blessed Spirits, more and more, Our de - vo-tion still in - creas-ing, As you fa-vours on us pour;

MICHAEL, PRINCE OF HIGHEST HEAVEN.

206. JESUS MY LORD, MY GOD, MY ALL.

FREDERICK WESTLAKE.

Jesus! my Lord, my God, my all! How can I love Thee as I ought? And how revere this wondrous gift, So far surpassing hope or thought? Sweet Sacrament! we Thee adore! O, make us love Thee more and more!

Had I but Mary's sinless heart To love Thee with, my dearest King! O with what bursts of fervent praise Thy goodness, Jesus, would I sing! Sweet Sacrament! we Thee adore! O, make us love Thee more and more!

Thy Body, Soul, and Godhead all!
O mystery of love divine!
I cannot compass all I have,
For all thou hast and art are mine!
Sweet Sacrament! we Thee adore!
O make us love Thee more and more.

Sound, sound His praise higher still,
Come all ye angels to our aid,
'Tis God! 'tis God! the very God,
Whose power both man and angels made!
Sweet Sacrament! we Thee adore!
O, make us love Thee more and more!

207. JESUS! MY LORD, MY GOD, MY ALL.

Had I but Mary's sinless heart
  To love Thee with, my dearest King!
O with what bursts of fervent praise
  Thy goodness, Jesus, would I sing
    Sweet Sacrament! we Thee adore!
    O, make us love Thee more and more!

O see! within a creature's hand
  The vast Creator deigns to be,
Reposing infant-like, as though
  On Joseph's arm, or Mary's knee.
    Sweet Sacrament! we Thee adore!
    O, make us love Thee more and more!

Thy Body, Soul, and Godhead, all!
  O mystery of love divine!
I cannot compass all I have,
  For all Thou hast and art are mine!
    Sweet Sacrament! we Thee adore!
    O, make us love Thee more and more!

Sound, sound His praises higher still,
  And come, ye angels, to our aid,
'Tis God! 'tis God! the very God,
  Whose power both man and angels made!
    Sweet Sacrament! we Thee adore!
    O, make us love Thee more and more!

Lest one heart that loves Him
E'er should sigh with pain,
Pining for His presence,
Seeking Him in vain,—
He on earth would tarry
Near to every one,
That each heart might find Him
On His altar-throne.

Jesus, food of angels!
Monarch of the heart,
Oh, that I could never
From Thy face depart!
Yes, Thou ever dwellest
Here for love of me,
Hidden Thou remainest,
God of Majesty!

Soon I hope to see Thee,
And enjoy Thy love,
Face to face, sweet Jesus,
In Thy heaven above.
But on earth an exile,
My delight shall be
Ever to be near Thee,
Veiled for love of me.

209. MY SOUL, WHAT DOST THOU. J. R. SCHACHNER.

My soul, what dost thou? Answer me—Love God who loves thee well:—Love only does He ask of thee, Canst thou His love repel? See, how on earth for love of thee, In lowly form of bread, The Sovereign Good and Majesty His dwelling-place has made.

He bids thee now His friendship prove, And at His table eat; To share the bread of life and love, His own true flesh thy meat. What other gift so great, so high, Could God Himself impart? Could love divine do more to buy The love of thy poor heart? A-men.

Though once, in agonies of pain,
Upon the cross He died,
A love so great, not even then
Was wholly satisfied.
Not till the hour when He had found
The sweet mysterious way
To join His heart in closest bond
To thy poor heart of clay

How, then, amid such ardent flame,
My soul, dost thou not burn?
Canst thou refuse, for very shame,
A loving heart's return?
Then yield thy heart, at length, to love
That God of Charity,
Who gives His very self to prove
The love He bears to thee!

210. O BREAD OF HEAVEN.

G. H.

O Bread of Heav'n! beneath this veil, .. Thou dost my very God .. conceal, .. My Jesus dearest treasure Hail! I love Thee, and .. adoring kneel. Each loving soul by Thee is fed With Thy own self in form of bread.

O Food of Life! Thou who dost give
  The pledge of immortality!
I live;—no, 'tis not I that live.
  God gives me life, God lives in me:
He feeds my soul, He guides my ways;
And every grief with joy repays.

O Bond of Love! that dost unite
  The servant to his loving Lord!
Could I dare live and not requite
  Such love,—then death were meet reward:
I cannot live unless to prove
Some love for such unmeasured love.

O mighty Fire! Thou that dost burn
  To kindle every mind and heart!
For Thee my frozen soul doth yearn;
  Come Lord of Love, thy warmth impart,
If thus to speak too bold appear,
'Tis love like thine has banished fear.

O sweetest Dart of Love Divine!
  If I have sinned, then vengeance take:
Come, pierce this guilty heart of mine,
  And let it die for His dear sake
Who once expired on Calvary,
His heart pierced through for love of me.

My dearest Good! who dost so bind
  My heart with countless chains to Thee!
O sweetest Love, my soul shall find
  In Thy dear bonds true liberty.
Thyself Thou hast bestowed on me,
Thine, thine for ever I will be!

Beloved Lord! In Heaven above,—
  There, Jesus, Thou awaitest me
To gaze on Thee with changeless love.
  Yes, thus I hope,—thus shall it be.
For how can He deny me heaven,
Who here on earth Himself hath given?

211. IN THIS SWEET SACRAMENT, TO THEE.

Come now, my loving Lord, to me,
Oh, come into my heart;
Inflame it all with love of Thee,
And never thence depart.
And let this wretched heart be thine,
Yes, thine, dear God, alone!
And, Mary, may this soul of mine
Henceforth be all Thy own!

So worship we God in those rude latter days;
So worship we Jesus, our Love, when we praise
His wonderful grace in the gifts He gave thee—
The gift of clear shining, sweet Star of the Sea!

Deep night hath come down on us, Mother! deep night,
We need more than ever the guide of thy light;
For the darker the night is, the brighter should be
Thy beautiful shining, sweet Star of the Sea!

213. MOTHER OF MERCY.

Ah, little know they of thy worth
Who would thy love deny to me;
For what did Jesus love on earth
One-half so tenderly as thee?

Oh, gain me grace to love thee more;
Thy Son will give if thou wilt plead:
And, Mother, when life's cares are o'er
Oh, I shall love thee then indeed.

My Lord, when His three hours were run,
Bequeath'd Thee from the cross to me;
And oh, how can I love thy Son,
Sweet Mother, if I love not thee?

214. O MAID CONCEIVED WITHOUT A STAIN.

Adapted from Hasse.

1. O maid conceiv'd with-out a stain, O mo-ther bright and fair, Come thou with-in our hearts to reign, And grace shall tri-umph there. Hail, Ma-ry, e-ver un-de-fil'd, Hail,
2. Thou art far pur-er than the snow, Far bright-er than the day; Thy beau-ty none on earth can know, No tongue of man can say. O mo-ther, of all mo-thers best, Who
3. O then for us, thy children, plead, Thy pi-ty we im-plore; That we from sin and sor-row freed, May love Thee more and more. Hail, Ma-ry, e-ver un-de-fil'd, Hail,

O MAID CONCEIVED WITHOUT A STAIN.

The following may be sung to the same music.—

Sweet Morn! thou parent of the sun,
   And daughter of the same,
What joy and gladness, through thy birth,
   This day to mortals came!
Cloth'd in the sun, I see thee stand,
   The moon beneath thy feet;
The stars above thy sacred head;
   A radiant coronet.

Dominions, thrones, around thee stand,
   The armies of the sky,
And streams of glory from thee flow,
   All bath'd in Deity!
Terrific as the banner'd line
   Of battle's dread array,
Before thee tremble hell and death,
   And own thy potent sway

Now crush'd beneath thy dauntless foot,
   The serpent writhes in vain;
Subdued for evermore, and bound
   In an eternal chain.
O Mightiest! pray for us, that He
   Who came through thee of yore,
May come to dwell within our hearts,
   And never quit us more.

MOTHER MARY.

Bro-ther Points to Ma-ry by His side. Thou wilt love us, thou wilt guide us, With a Mother's fond-est care; And our Fa-ther, God a-bove us, Bids us fly for re-fuge there. Life's temp-ta-tions are be-fore us, We must min-gle in the strife; If thy

sta-tion Close to Je-sus in the skies. Mo-ther Ma-ry, to thy keep-ing We our-selves to thee con-fide; Toil-ing, rest-ing, wak-ing, sleep-ing, To be e-ver at thy side. Cares that vex us, joys that please us, Life and death we trust to thee; Thou wilt

216. HAIL, OCEAN STAR!

Break thou the chain
Of those whom sin has bound;
Upon the blind thy radiance pour,
Each ill remove, each bliss implore:
Hail, Mary, hail!

Show, show thyself
The Mother that thou art;
Present our prayers before His throne,
Who for our sake became thy Son:
Hail, Mary, hail!

O Virgin blest,
O meekest of the meek!
Keep us in virtue's path secure;
Keep us, O keep us, meek and pure:
Hail, Mary, hail!

Be thou the guide
Of all our life, we pray,
Till in thy bosom safe we rest,
With Christ's eternal vision blest
Hail, Mary, hail!

No. 217, *Accompaniment*, see No. 130.

Hymns and Sacred Songs.

Part III.

containing

HYMNS, CHIEFLY IN UNISON, FOR SCHOOLS.
MISSIONS, STATIONS OF THE CROSS, &c.

WITH ORGAN ACCOMPANIMENT.

218. ST. JOSEPH TO THE INFANT JESUS.

Adapted from STIASTNY.

"Je-sus! let me call thee Son, Since Thou dost call me fa-ther;

How I love Thee, sweet-est One! My God and Son to-ge-ther."

Bles-sed St. Jo-seph! to thee do we pray, Of-fer our hearts to thy Je-sus to-day.

"As my God I Thee adore,
  And as my Son embrace Thee;
Let me love Thee more and more,
  And in my bosom place Thee."
    Blessed St. Joseph! &c.

"Since Thy guardian I must be,
  My treasure I will make Thee;
Do not Thou abandon me,
  And I will ne'er forsake Thee."
    Blessed St. Joseph! &c.

"All my love henceforth is Thine,
  My very life I proffer,
And my heart no more is mine,
  For all I am I offer."
    Blessed St. Joseph! &c.

"Since to share Thy presence sweet
  To choose me here Thou deignest;
Shall we not in heaven meet,
  Where Thou for ever reignest?"
    Blessed St. Joseph! &c.

No. 219, *Accompaniment*, see No. 214.

220. HAIL! HOLY JOSEPH.

G. H.

Hail! holy Joseph, hail!
Father of Christ esteem'd!
Father be thou to those
Thy Foster Son redeem'd!

Hail! holy Joseph, hail!
Prince of the house of God!
May His best graces be
By thy sweet hands bestow'd.

Hail! holy Joseph, hail!
Belov'd of angels, hail!
Cheer thou the hearts that faint
And guide the steps that fail.

Hail! holy Joseph, hail!
God's choice wert thou alone;
To thee the Lord made flesh
Was subject as a Son.

Hail! holy Joseph, hail!
Teach us our flesh to tame;
And, Mary, keep the hearts
That love thy husband's name.

Mother of Jesus! bless,
And bless, ye Saints on high,
All meek and simple souls
That to St. Joseph cry.

221. THE HOLY FAMILY.

G. H.

1. Hap-py we, who thus u-ni-ted Join in cheer-ful me-lo-dy,
Prais-ing Jesus, Mary, Joseph. In the "Ho-ly Fa-mi-ly."
Jesus, Mary, Joseph, help us That we e-ver true may be
To the pro-mi-ses that bind us To the "Ho-ly Fa-mi-ly." A-men.

2. Jesus, whose Al-migh-ty bid-ding All crea-a-ted things ful-fil,
Lives on earth in meek sub-jec-tion To His earth-ly pa-rent's will.
Sweet-est In-fant! make us pa-tient, And o-be-dient for Thy sake;
Teach us to be chaste and gen-tle, All our stor-my pas-sions break.

Mary! thou alone wert chosen
To be Mother of thy Lord:
Thou didst guide the early footsteps
Of the Great Incarnate Word.

Dearest Mother! make us humble,
For thy Son will take His rest
In the poor and lowly dwelling
Of an humble sinner's breast.

Joseph! thou wert called the Father
Of thy Maker and thy Lord,
Thine it was to save thy Saviour
From the cruel Herod's sword.

Suffer us to call thee Father,
Shew to us a father's love;
Lead us safe through every danger
Till we meet in heaven above.

ACT OF CONTRITION.

ENGLISH MELODY ADAPTED.

By my sins I have deserved
　Death and endless misery;
Hell with all its pains and torments,
　And for all eternity!
　　　　Jesus! Lord! I ask for mercy, &c.

By my sins I have abandoned,
　Right and claim to Heaven above;
Where the Saints rejoice for ever
　In a boundless sea of love.
　　　　Jesus! Lord! I ask for mercy, &c.

See our Saviour, bleeding, dying,
　On the Cross of Calvary,
To that Cross my sins have nailed Him,
　Yet He bleeds and dies for me.
　　　　Jesus! Lord! I ask for mercy, &c.

223. DEAR ANGEL! EVER AT MY SIDE.

(FOR CHILDREN.)

GIULIO ROBERTI.

But when, dear Spirit! I kneel down
At morn and night, to prayer,
There is a voice within my heart
Which tells me thou art there.
Yes! when I pray thou prayest too,
Thy prayer is all for me,
And when I sleep, thou sleepest not,
But watchest patiently.

Then, for thy sake, dear Angel! now
More humble will I be,
But I am weak, and when I fall,
O weary not of me;
O, love me still, sweet angel guide
And I will love thee more;
And help me when my soul is cast
Upon th' eternal shore.

Words in "Hymns for the Year," No. 240.

225.   I'LL NEVER FORSAKE THEE!

Words in "Hymns for the Year," No. 231.

O FLOWER OF GRACE.

228. HYMN TO ST. AGNES.

1. Sweet Agnes, holy child, All purity; O, may we undefil'd, Be pure as Thee. Ready our blood to shed, Forth as the martyrs led, Their path of pain to tread, And die like Thee!
2. O, gentle patroness, Of holy youth; Ask God all those to bless, Who love the truth. O guide us on our way, Unto th'eternal day, With hearts all pure and gay, Dear saint like Thine!
3. Look down and hear our pray'r, From realms above; Show us Thy tender care, Thy guiding love. O keep us in Thy sight, Till in th'unclouded light Of heav'n's pure vision bright, We dwell with Thee!

F. W.

Words in "Hymns for the Year," No. 275.

229. O THOU, THE MARTYR'S GLORIOUS KING.

O Thou, the Martyr's glorious King, Of Confessors the crown and prize, Who dost to joys celestial bring Those who the joys of earth despise, Those who the joys of earth despise, Amen.

Words in "Hymns for the year," No. 144.

230. FROM PAIN TO PAIN
(GOOD FRIDAY, OR STATIONS.)

231. NOW ARE THE DAYS OF HUMBLEST PRAYER.
(LENT.)

Words in Hymns for the year, No. 217.

232. YE SONS AND DAUGHTERS OF THE LORD.

Alleluia! Alleluia! Alleluia!

Ye sons and daughters of the Lord, The King of heav'n, the King a-
O Fi - li - i et Fi - li - æ, Rex cœ - les - tis, Rex Glo - ri -

-dor'd, From death this day Him-self restor'd.   Al - - - le - lu - ia!
- æ, Mor - te sur - rex - it ho - di - e.

Alleluia! Alleluia! Al - - - le - lu - ia.

Words in "Hymns for the Year," No. 237.

233. HOLY SPIRIT, LORD OF LIGHT.

Ho-ly Spi-rit, Lord of Light, From Thy clear ce - les - tial light, Thy pure beaming ra-diance give. Come, thou Fa-ther
Ve-ni Sancte Spi - ri - tus, Et e - mit - te cœ - li - tus, Lu-cis tu - œ ra - di - um. Ve - ni Pa - ter

of the poor, Come with treasures which endure, Come, thou light of all that live.   A-men Al-le-lu - - - ia.
pau - per - um, Ve - ni da - tor mu - nerum, Ve - ni lu - men cor - di - um.

Words in "Hymns for the Year," No. 212.

234. COME ALL YE FAITHFUL.

Adeste fideles,
Læti triumphantes;
Venite, venite in Bethlehem:
Natum videte
Regem angelorum:
Venite adoremus,
Venite adoremus,
Venite adoremus Dominum.

Deum de Deo,
Lumen de lumine,
Gestant puellæ viscera:
Deum verum,
Genitum, non factum:
    Venite adoremus, &c.

Cantet nunc Io!
Chorus angelorum:
Cantet nunc aula cœlestium,
Gloria
In excelsis Deo!
    Venite, &c.

Ergo qui natus
Die hodierna,
Jesu tibi sit gloria:
Patris æterni
Verbum caro factum!
Venite adoremus,
Venite adoremus,
Venite adoremus Domin...

Come, all ye faithful,
    Joyful and triumphant,
O hasten, O hasten to Bethlehem;
    See in a manger
The Monarch of angels.
        O come and let us worship Christ the
            Lord.

God of God eternal,
    Light from light proceeding,
He deigns in the Virgin's womb to lie;
    Very God of very God,
Begotten not created.
    O come, &c.

Sing alleluia,
    All ye choirs of angels;
Sing, all ye citizens of heaven above,
    Glory to God
In the highest,
    O come, &c.

Yea, Lord, we greet Thee,
    Born this happy morning,
To Thee, O Jesus, be glory given;
    True Word of the Father,
In our flesh appearing.
    O come, &c.

CHRISTIANS! TO THE WAR!

Words in "Hymns for the Year," No. 245.

236. THE STATIONS OF THE CROSS.

Ho-ly mother, pierce me through, In my heart each wound renew, Of my Sa-viour cru-ci-fied.
Sancta ma-ter is-tud a-gas, Cru-ci-fix-i fi-ge pla-gas, Cor-di me-o va-li-de.

237. O COME AND MOURN.

O come and mourn with me a-while, See, Ma-ry calls us to her side; O come and let us mourn with her, Je-sus our love is cru-ci-fied. A-men.

Words in "Hymns for the Year," No. 105, also for Nos. 26, 39.

238. O GODHEAD HID.

O God-head hid, de-vout-ly I a-dore Thee, Who tru-ly art with-in the forms be-fore me, To Thee my heart I bow with bend-ed knee, As fail-ing quite in con-tem-pla-ting Thee.

Words in "Hymns for the Year," No. 158.

239. GREEN ARE THE LEAVES.

Words in "Hymns for the Year," No. 225.

240. O'ERWHELMED IN DEPTHS OF WOE.

Words in "Hymns for the Year," No. 27.

241. DEAR ANGEL! EVER AT MY SIDE.

Hymns for the Year, No. 188.

242. O THOU, THE MARTYRS' GLORIOUS KING!

Hymns for the Year, No. 141 and 105.

243. THE MOON IS IN THE HEAVENS ABOVE.

Hymns for the Year, No. 121 and 119.

244. HAPPY WE WHO THUS UNITED.

Hymns for the Year, No. 187; also for St. Casimir's Hymn, 132, 133.

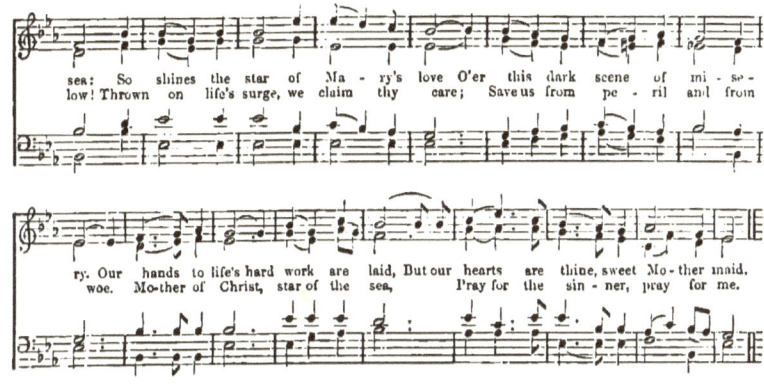

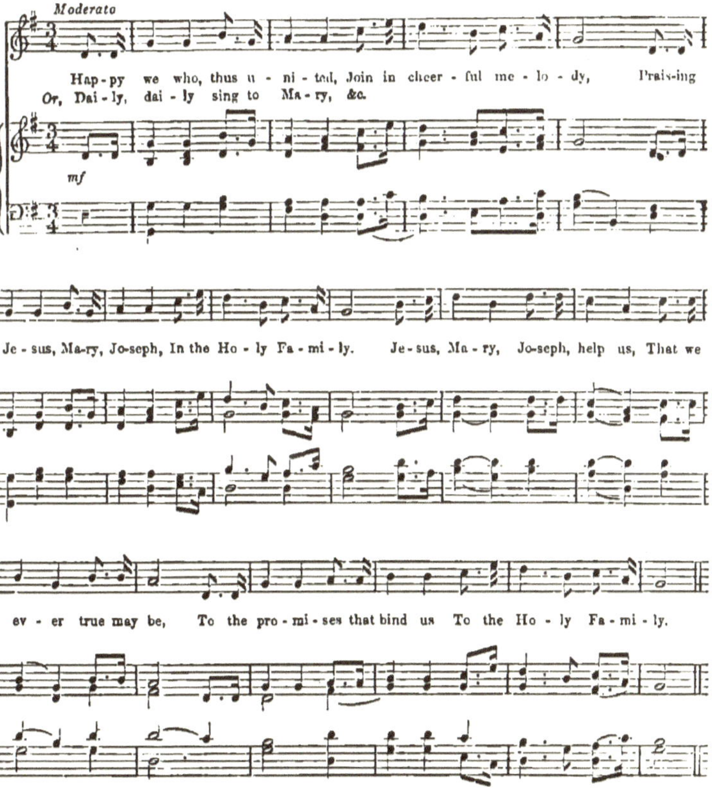

245. THERE IS ONE TRUE AND ONLY GOD.

There is one true and only God, Our Maker and our Lord; And He created ev'ry thing, By His Almighty Word. All this and all the Church doth teach, My God, I do believe; For Thou hast bid us hear the Church, And Thou canst not deceive.

Words in Hymns for the Year, No. 241.

246. GREAT GOD, WHATEVER THROUGH THY CHURCH.

Great God, whatever through Thy Church, Thou teachest to be true; I firmly do believe it all, And will confess it too. Thou never canst deceived be, Thou never canst deceive, For Thou art truth itself, and Thou Dost tell me to believe. Amen.

Words in Hymns for the Year, No. 243.

247. HAVE MERCY ON US, GOD MOST HIGH.

Words in Hymns for the Year, No. 1.

248. COME, O CREATOR SPIRIT BLEST.

Words in Hymns for the Year, No. 14.

249. MY GOD I LOVE THEE.

J. Richardson.

Words in Hymns for the Year, No. 81.

250. HAIL, BRIGHT STAR OF OCEAN.

Words in Hymns for the Year, No. 115.

251. HAIL, BRIGHT STAR OF OCEAN.

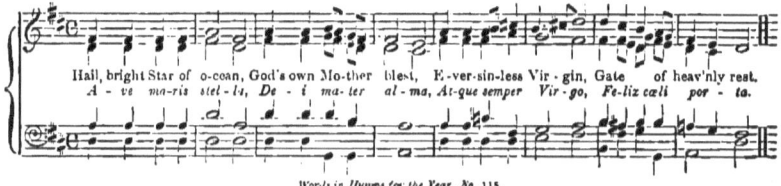

Words in Hymns for the Year, No. 115.

252. MOTHER OF MERCY.

Words in Hymns for the Year, No. 117.

253. HOLY QUEEN, WE BEND BEFORE THEE.

J. Richardson

Words in Hymns for the Year, No. 133.

254. HAIL, HOLY JOSEPH.

* The Melody ends here.   Words in Hymns for the Year, No. 140.

255. JESUS, THE VERY THOUGHT OF THEE.

J. RICHARDSON.

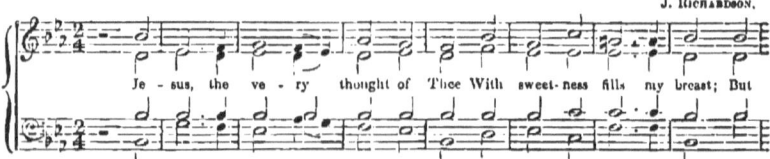
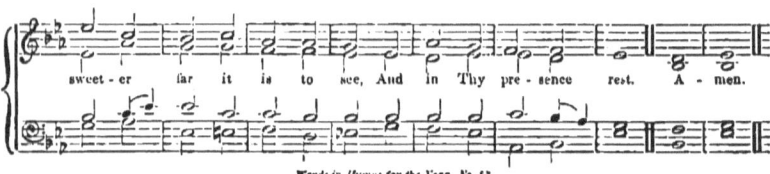

Jesus, the very thought of Thee With sweetness fills my breast; But sweeter far it is to see, And in Thy presence rest. A-men.

Words in Hymns for the Year, No. 57.

256. O JESUS, GOD AND MAN.

H. RICHARDSON.

O Jesus, God and man, for love Of children once a child; O Jesus, God and man, we hail Thee Saviour meek and mild. A-men.

Words in Hymns for the Year, No. 256.

257. OH! WHAT IS THIS ENCHANTING CALM?

J. RICHARDSON.

Adagio.

Oh! what is this enchanting calm, Which now with peace my bosom fills, Which o'er my spirit pours a balm, And thro' my inmost being thrills? A-men.

Words in Hymns for the Year, No. 255.

258. O FLOWERS, O HAPPY FLOWERS.

Words in Hymns for the Year, No. 250.

259. THOU LOVING MAKER OF MANKIND.

1. Thou lov-ing Ma-ker of man-kind, Be-fore Thy throne we pray and weep; O strength-en us with grace di-vine, Du-ly this sa-cred time to keep.
2. Great Judge of hearts, Thou dost our ills Dis-cern, and all our weak-ness know; A-gain to Thee with tears we turn, A-gain to us Thy mer-cy show. A-men.

Words in "Hymns for the Year," No. 26.

260. COMPLINE HYMN.

1. Now with the fast-de-par-ting light, Ma-ker of all, we ask of Thee, Of Thy great mer-cy, thro' the night Our guar-dian and de-fence to be.
2. Far off let i-dle vi-sions fly, No phan-tom of the night mo-lest; Curb Thou our ra-ging e-ne-my, That we in chaste re-pose may rest.
3. Fa-ther of mer-cies, hear our cry, Hear us, O sole-be-got-ten Son, Who, with the Ho-ly Ghost most high, Reign-est while end-less a-ges run. A-men.

Words in "Hymns for the Year," No. 89.

261. O BLEST CREATOR OF THE LIGHT.

PLEYEL.

264. WHAT LIGHT IS STREAMING FROM THE SKIES?

1. What light is stream-ing from the skies, Re-veal-ing Heaven to mor-tal eyes? What voice is sing-ing from the spheres An-gel-ic hymns to mor-tal ears? A-men.

2. O ho-liest mys-te-ry of love! From His re-splen-dent throne a-bove The Sa-viour comes, un-seen, to dwell With-in the hearts He loves so well. A-men.

3.
Each soul becomes His happy guest;
A heav'nly joy now fills the breast;
All earthly thoughts have fled away,
As night before th' approach of day.

4.
New virtues in us shall abound,
Like flowers of spring in goodly ground;
The Lord is with us; His right arm
Shall guard our future life from harm.

265. LIGHT OF THE SOUL.

R. Brown.*

1. Light of the soul, O Sa-viour blest, Soon as Thy pres-ence fills the breast Dark-ness and guilt are put to flight, And all is sweet-ness and de-light. A-men.

2. Son of the Fa-ther, Lord most high, How glad is he who feels Thee nigh! How sweet in heav'n Thy beam doth glow, De-nied to eye of flesh be-low. A-men.

3.
O Light of light celestial,
O Charity ineffable;
Come in Thy hidden majesty;
Fill us with love, fill us with Thee.

4.
To Jesus from the proud conceal'd,
But evermore to babes reveal'd,
All glory with the Father be,
And Holy Ghost eternally.

* From the " Supplemental Hymn and Tune Book " (by permission.)

SWEET SAVIOUR, BLESS US ERE WE GO.

RICHARDSON.

1. Sweet Saviour! bless us ere we go; Thy word into our minds instil; And make our lukewarm hearts to glow With lowly love, and fervent will. Through life's long day and death's dark night, O, gentle Jesus, be our light! Amen.

2. The day is done, its hours have run; And Thou hast taken count of all,— The scanty triumphs grace has won, The broken vow, the frequent fall. Through life's long day, &c.

3.
Grant us, dear Lord! from evil ways
True absolution and release;
And bless us more than in past days
With purity and inward peace.
    Through life's long day, &c.

4.
Do more than pardon,—give us joy,
Sweet fear and sober liberty;
And simple hearts without alloy,
That only long to be like Thee.
    Through life's long day, &c.

5.
Labour is sweet, for Thou hast toiled;
And care is light, for Thou hast cared:
Ah! never let our works be soiled
With strife, or by deceit ensnared.
    Through life's long day, &c.

6.
For all we love, the poor, the sad,
The sinful,—unto Thee we call;
Oh, let Thy mercy make us glad:
Thou art our Jesus and our All!
    Through life's long day, &c.

EVENING HYMN.

T. G. Parry.

1. O blest Creator of the light, Who dost the dawn from darkness bring, framing Nature's depth and height, Didst with the new-born light begin; Amen.

2. Who, gently blending eve with morn, And morn with eve, didst call them Day; Thick flows the flood of darkness down; O hear us as we weep and pray.

3.
Keep Thou our souls from schemes of crime,
 Nor guilt remorseful let them know;
Nor, thinking but on things of time,
 Into eternal darkness go.

4.
Teach us to knock at Heaven's high door,
 Teach us the prize of life to win;
Teach us all evil to abhor,
 And purify ourselves within.

5.
Father of mercies! hear our cry;
 Hear us, O sole-begotten Son!
Who, with the Holy Ghost most high,
 Reignest while endless ages run.

Or this.

1.
O Thou true life of all that live,
 Who dost, unmoved, all motion sway;
Who dost the morn and evening give,
 And through its changes guide the day;

2.
Thy light upon our evening pour;
 So may our souls no sunset see:
But death to us an open door
 To an eternal morning be.

3.
Father of mercies, hear our cry;
 Hear us, O sole-begotten Son,
Who, with the Holy Ghost most high,
 Reignest while endless ages run.

* *From the Supplemental Hymn Book.* (as 265).

268. HARK! AN AWFUL VOICE IS SOUNDING.

R. Haking.*

1. Hark! an awful voice is sounding; "Christ is nigh," it seems to say;
"Cast away the dreams of darkness, O ye children of the day!"
Startled at the solemn warning, Let the earth-bound soul arise;
Christ her Sun, all sloth dispelling, Shines upon the morning skies.

2. Lo, the Lamb so long expected, Comes with pardon down from heav'n;
Let us haste with tears of sorrow, One and all to be forgiv'n,
So when next He comes with glory, Wrapping all the earth in fear,
May He then, as our defender, On the clouds of heav'n appear! A-men.

JESUS, LORD, BE THOU MY OWN.

(To the same Music.)

Jesus, Lord, be Thou my own;
Thee I long for, Thee alone;
All myself I give to Thee;
Do whate'er Thou wilt with me.

Life without Thy love would be
Death, O Sovereign Good, to me;
Bound and held by Thy dear chains,
Captive now my heart remains.

Thou, O God, my heart inflame,
Give that love which Thou dost claim;
Payment I will ask for none;
Love demands but love alone.

God of beauty, Lord of light,
Thy good will is my delight;
Now henceforth Thy will divine
Ever shall in all be mine.

* *From the Supplemental Hymn Book (as 263).*

269. O JESU, SAVIOUR OF THE WORLD.

Words in Hymns for the Year, No. 20.

270. JESU, CREATOR OF THE WORLD.

Words in Hymns for the Year, No. 18.

271. O CHRIST, THY GUILTY PEOPLE SPARE.

Words in Hymns for the Year, No. 120.

272. THE SHADOWS OF THE EVENING HOURS.

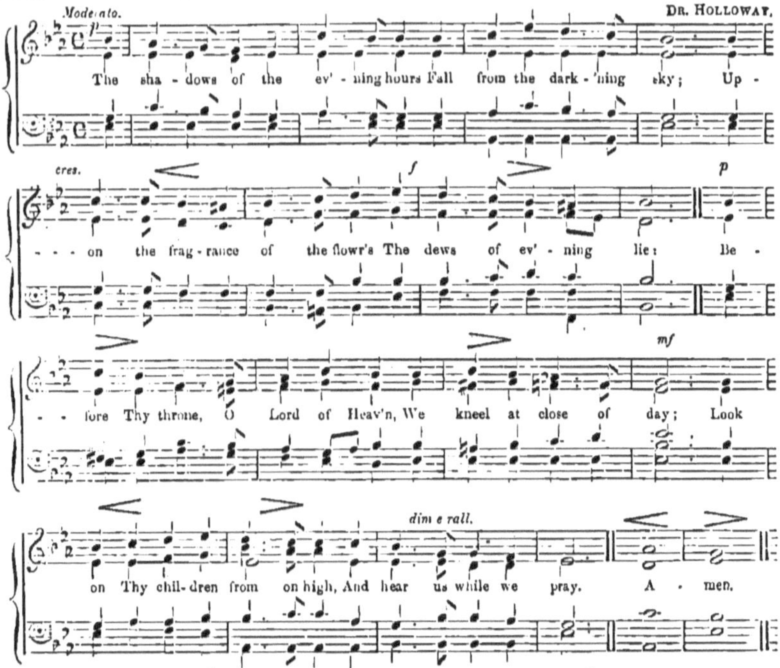
Moderato.
Dr. Holloway.
The sha - dows of the ev' - ning hours Fall from the dark - 'ning sky; Up -
cres.
f
p
- on the frag - rance of the flowr's The dews of ev' - ning lie: Be -
mf
- fore Thy throne, O Lord of Heav'n, We kneel at close of day; Look
dim e rall.
on Thy chil - dren from on high, And hear us while we pray. A - men.

2.

The sorrows of Thy servants, Lord,
O do not Thou despise;
But let the incense of our prayers
Before Thy mercy rise.
The brightness of the coming night
Upon the darkness rolls;
With hopes of future glory chase
The shadows on our souls.

3.

Let peace, O Lord, Thy peace, O God,
Upon our souls descend;
From midnight fears and perils Thou
Our trembling hearts defend.
Give us a respite from our toil;
Calm and subdue our woes;
Through the long day we suffer, Lord,
O give us now repose.

273. COME, O CREATOR SPIRIT BLEST. (*Unison.*)

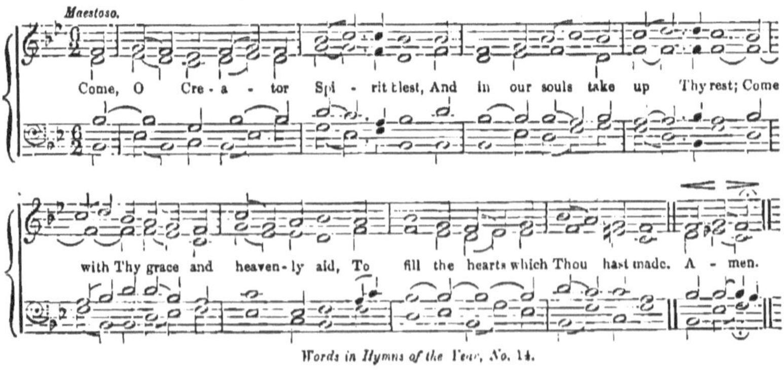
Maestoso.
Come, O Cre - a - tor Spi - rit blest, And in our souls take up Thy rest; Come
with Thy grace and heaven - ly aid, To fill the hearts which Thou hast made. A - men.

Words in Hymns of the Year, No. 14.

274. THERE IS ONE TRUE AND ONLY GOD.

Words in Hymns of the Year, No 241.

275. AS FADES THE GLOWING ORB OF DAY.

276. WHEN MORNING GILDS THE SKIES.

W. A. Barrett.

2.
The sacred minster-bell,
It peals o'er hill and dell,
  May Jesus Christ be prais'd!
Oh, hark to what it sings,
As joyously it rings,
  May Jesus Christ be prais'd!

3.
When you begin the day,
Oh, never fail to say,
  May Jesus Christ be prais'd!
And at your work rejoice
To sing with heart and voice,
  May Jesus Christ be prais'd!

4.
Be this at meals your grace,
In every time and place,
  May Jesus Christ be prais'd!
Be this when day is past,
Of all your thoughts the last,
  May Jesus Christ be prais'd!

5.
To God the Word on high
The hosts of angels cry,
  May Jesus Christ be prais'd!
Let children too upraise
Their voice in hymns of praise;
  May Jesus Christ be prais'd!

6.
Let earth's wide circle round
In joyful notes resound:
  May Jesus Christ be prais'd!
Let air and sea and sky,
Through depth and height reply:
  May Jesus Christ be prais'd!

277. NOW LET THE EARTH WITH JOY RESOUND.

BEETHOVEN.

Words in Hymns for the Year, No. 255.

278. O THOU OF ALL THY WARRIORS, LORD.

HAYDN.

Words in Hymns for the Year, No. 257.

279. LOOK DOWN, O MOTHER MARY.

J. HALLETT SHEPPARD.

1. Look down, O Mother Mary, From thy bright throne above; Cast down upon thy children One only glance of love; And if a heart so tender, With pity flows not o'er, Then turn away, O Mother, And look on us no more.

2. See how, ungrateful sinners, We stand before thy Son; His loving heart upbraids us The evil we had done. But if thou wilt appease Him, Speak for us but one word; Thou only canst obtain us The pardon of our Lord. Amen.

3.
O Mary, dearest Mother,
  If thou wouldst have us live,
Say that we are thy children,
  And Jesus will forgive.
Our sins make us unworthy
  That title still to bear,
But thou art still our Mother;
  Then show a Mother's care.

4.
Unfold to us thy mantle;
  There stay we without fear,
What evil can befal us
  If, Mother, thou art near?
O kindest, dearest Mother,
  Thy sinful children save;
Look down on us with pity,
  Who thy protection crave.

280. WHEN THE LOVING SHEPHERD.

J. HALLETT SHEPPARD.

1. When the loving Shepherd, Ere He left the earth,
Shed, to pay our ransom, Blood of priceless worth,—
These His lambs so cherish'd, Purchas'd for His own,
He would not abandon In the world alone.

2. Ere He makes us partners Of His realm on high,
Happy and immortal With Him in the sky,—
Love immense, stupendous, Makes him here below
Partner of our exile In this world of woe. Amen.

3.
Jesus, food of angels,
  Monarch of the heart;
O, that I could never
  From Thy face depart!
Yes, Thou ever dwellest
  Here for love of me,
Hidden Thou remainest,
  God of Majesty.

4.
Soon I hope to see Thee,
  And enjoy Thy love,
Face to face, sweet Jesus
  In Thy heaven above.
But on earth an exile,
  My delight shall be
Ever to be near Thee,
  Veiled for love of me

This tune may also be used for No. 216, "Jesus, gentlest Saviour."

281. AT THE CROSS HER STATION KEEPING.

2.

Oh, how sad and sore distressèd
Now was she, that Mother blessèd
  Of the sole-begotten One!
Woe-begone, with heart's prostration,
Mother meek, the bitter passion
  Saw she of her glorious Son.

3.

Who could mark, from tears refraining,
Christ's dear Mother uncomplaining,
  In so great a sorrow bow'd?
Who, unmov'd, behold her languish
Underneath His Cross of anguish,
  Mid the fierce unpitying crowd?

4.

In His people's sins rejected,
She her Jesus, unprotected,
  Saw with thorns, with scourges rent:
Saw her Son from judgment taken,
Her belov'd in death forsaken,
Till His spirit forth He sent.

282. NONE OF ALL THE NOBLEST CITIES.

2.
By its rays divinely guided,
  See the Eastern kings appear ;
See them bend their gifts to offer,
  Gifts of incense, gold, and myrrh.
Sacred types of mystic meaning :
  Incense doth the God disclose,
Gold a royal Child proclaimeth,
  Myrrh a future tomb foreshows.

3.
Holy Jesu, in Thy brightness
  To the Gentile world reveal'd,
Still to babes Thyself disclosing,
  Ever from the proud conceal'd.
Honour, glory, virtue, merit,
  Be to Thee, O Virgin's Son,
With the Father and the Spirit,
  While eternal ages run.

283. HAIL! HOLY JOSEPH, HAIL!

G. H.

2
Hail, holy Joseph, hail!
Prince of the House of God;
May His best graces be
By thy sweet hands bestow'd.

3
Hail, holy Joseph, hail!
Belov'd of angels, hail;
Cheer thou the hearts that faint,
And guide the steps that fail.

4
Hail, holy Joseph, hail!
God's choice wert thou alone;
To thee the Word made flesh
Was subject as a Son.

5
Hail, holy Joseph, hail!
Teach us our flesh to tame;
And, Mary, keep the hearts
That love thy husband's name.

6
Mother of Jesus, bless,
And bless, ye Saints on high,
All meek and simple souls
That to St. Joseph cry.

284. NOW WITH THE FAST-DEPARTING LIGHT.

J. HALLETT SHEPHERD.

2.
Far off let idle visions fly,
No phantom of the night molest;
Curb Thou our raging enemy,
That we in chaste repose may rest.

3.
Father of mercies, hear our cry;
Hear us, O sole-begotten Son,
Who, with the Holy Ghost most high,
Reignest while endless ages run.

285. AS FADES THE GLOWING ORB OF DAY.

ARRANGED BY J. HALLETT SHEPHERD.

288. ALL YE WHO SEEK A SURE RELIEF.

289. TO CHRIST, THE PRINCE OF PEACE.

2.
O Jesu, Victim blest,
  What else but love divine
Could Thee constrain to open thus
  That sacred Heart of Thine ?
O Fount of endless life,
  O Spring of waters clear,
O Flame celestial, cleansing all
  Who unto Thee draw near :

3.
Hide me in Thy dear Heart,
  For thither do I fly ;
There seek Thy grace through life, in death
  Thine immortality.
Praise to the Father be,
  Praise to His only Son,
Praise to the blessed Paraclete,
  While endless ages run.

www.ingramcontent.com/pod-product-compliance
Lightning Source LLC
Chambersburg PA
CBHW030738230426
43667CB00007B/763